sonny rollins

Peter N. Wilson

sonny rollins

the definitive musical guide

berkeley hills books
berkeley california

Published by Berkeley Hills Books
PO Box 9877, Berkeley CA 94709

Discography translated by Emily Banwell

Library of Congress Cataloging-in-Publication Data

Wilson, Peter Niklas.
[Sonny Rollins. English]
Sonny Rollins : the definitive musical guide / by Peter Niklas Wilson.
p. cm.
Translation of: Sonny Rollins : sein Leben, seine Musik, seine Schallplatten.
Discography: p.
Includes bibliographical references (p.) and index.
ISBN 1-893163-06-7
1. Rollins, Sonny. 2. Rollins, Sonny—Discography. 3. Jazz musicians—United States—Biography. I. Title.
ML419.R64 W513 2001
788.7'165'092—dc21

2001002162

Distributed to the trade by Publishers Group West

contents

preface

"The greatest living improviser," "the greatest jazz musician alive," "the king of tenor players": three epithets regularly bestowed on Sonny Rollins by jazz journalists and jazz fans. Sonny Rollins, an all-time jazz great—that's the general consensus. Yet comparatively little is known about the life and music of this remarkable man. Sure enough, every jazz aficionado knows Rollins' jubilant calypso "St. Thomas" or has heard seminal Rollins records like *Saxophone Colossus* and *Way Out West.* But how many have followed Rollins on his erratic path through the '60s and beyond—how many know more about the man behind the music? This comparative obscurity is certainly Rollins' making to a great degree. For Walter Theodore (or Theodore Walter) Rollins is a withdrawn individual who avoids the media limelight, one who values his privacy, a person, too, who refuses to compromise his music for the sake of commercialism or mere trendiness.

This book does not pretend to be a full-length biography of Sonny Rollins. Rollins himself has announced that he intends to write his autobiography, and, in his book *Open Sky–Sonny Rollins and his World of Improvisation* Eric Nisenson has assembled a valuable biographical sketch from interviews with the saxophonist. The present volume, originally published in German in 1991 as part of the book series *Collection Jazz* and extensively revised and updated for this edition, is intended as a practical introduction to Rollins, the man and Rollins, the musician. As in my book on Ornette Coleman, a strong emphasis is on the artist's discographical oeuvre: the annotated discography tells the story of the musician's stylistic evolution and helps to make choices among the large number of available (and deleted) releases. The musical information is augmented by a chapter dealing with certain aspects of Rollins' music in more analytical detail. For the biographical chapters, I have drawn both on the substantial number of articles and interviews published since the late '50s and on my own lengthy interview with Sonny Rollins, which was conducted in Hamburg in 1987. Uncredited Rollins quotes are from this interview, parts of which were published in the German jazz review "Jazzthetik."

It is my hope that this book will help convey a more rounded, multi-faceted image of the artist Sonny Rollins, too often portrayed merely as a virtuoso hard bop player.

Peter Niklas Wilson
Hamburg, February 2001

biography

sonny boy from sugar hill (1930–1955)

A more favorable climate for a developing jazz musician would be hard to imagine. In the '30s and '40s Harlem was the center of black musical culture. Variety theaters such as the Apollo on 125th St., dance halls like the Savoy Ballroom (Lenox Avenue/140th Street), and music clubs like Minton's (118th Street) and Monroe's (134th Street) presented the full range of entertainment up to the comparatively esoteric innovations of bebop. The legendary Cotton Club was also here, at the intersection of Lenox Ave and West 142nd Street—until 1936 anyway, when this haunt of affluent white nightclubbers was transferred downtown after racial clashes to the "safer" confines of 48th Street.

Just a few blocks south of the Cotton Club, on the corner of Lenox and 137th, Walter Theodore Rollins was born September 7, 1930. (Rollins would later switch the official sequence of his first two names). In his early years his family changed addresses within the neighborhood several times: from 137th to 138th St., then to 135th and 136th– finally to settle in 1939 in an apartment on 153rd St. in the Sugar Hill area, at that time Harlem's most elegant neighborhood. This is where renowned jazz musicians like Don Redman lived, as well as Nat King Cole, Andy Kirk and–most significantly for Rollins–Coleman Hawkins. And so the Rollinses were numbered among the comparatively wealthy black bourgeoisie–in Sonny's own words: "middle class, with a piano in the living room and everything..." (Davis 1986, 123) His mother worked as domestic help for some rich white families on Park Avenue; his father, Walter Theodore Rollins Sr., was chief petty officer in the Navy, and would have advanced much farther in his career, Rollins believes, had it not been for his race: "I used to go down to Annapolis when I was a boy to spend time with him. He had an officer's club there. There would be admirals coming in. They entered the service the same time as my dad, and they were all friends with him, which gives you the idea he was of the caliber to make it if he hadn't been black." (West 1974, 24)

His parents were both originally from St. Thomas in the Virgin Islands, and both contributed to the family's musical life. Rollins' father played clarinet, his mother took him to dances where he heard calypso and Caribbean tunes. Walter Theodore Rollins was no prodigy, however. The obligatory piano lessons he started at eight or nine were soon terminated. "I just didn't make it. I was always sort of the black sheep of the family. I was out on the street playing ball so I never actually got into it." (Berg 1977, 13) His two older siblings fared better. Both sister and brother attended the Music and Art High School, an elite academy for the artistically gifted. His violinist brother even got an offer to become a member of the Pittsburgh Symphony Orchestra (which he declined in favor of a medical career). "My brother had a big influence on me, he practiced his violin all the time and some of that seeped into me when I was very young." (Blancq 1983, 3)

The tradition of European classical music, however, did not appeal to Rollins as much as the popular culture that surrounded him. Little Walter Theodore would pass longingly by the Savoy Ballroom and Cotton Club. "I used to walk by them both, wishing I could go inside. You didn't have to be grown to go to the Apollo, though, so I went down there at least once a week and caught practically everybody–Lionel Hampton, Fletcher Henderson, Duke Ellington, Count Basie... We used to see those guys do the stage show, then there'd be a movie. Boy, those were the days: go get some candy, see maybe a murder mystery. You'd hear the guys warming up in the background, and then you'd actually see them. You caught a great show." (Blumenthal 1979, 57) An uncle who owned records by blues artists Lonnie Johnson, Arthur Big Boy Crudup and jump star Louis Jordan, and an older cousin who played saxophone, soon exerted a greater influence than his brother and sister with their violin and piano. Singer and saxophonist Jordan, leader of the Tympany Five, and creator of a unique rhythm-and-blues idiom, was an especial favorite. "In my neighborhood, right beside the school, there was a cabaret/nightclub in my neighborhood called Barron's, adjacent to my grade school [134th St. and 7th Avenue]. Louis Jordan used to play there, and on the way to school I'd see these eight-by-ten glossies of him in the window with his King Zephyr alto sax. I really liked the look of that, and it stuck in my mind, always. I must've first seen those pictures when I was eight. A couple of years later, I had his early Decca sides around the house, like 'Knock Me A Kiss' and 'Five Guys Named Moe.' I loved his tone, his whole sound." (Cioe 1983, 77)

Rollins insists that the sheer visual impact of the gleaming saxophone also drew him to it. In 1942, his mother bought him his first instrument, a used alto. He took some lessons on 48th St., the district of the music business and private academies, but remained at bottom an autodidact. He had the opportunity to advance his knowledge by playing with others; among his classmates at Benjamin Franklin High School were the young pianist Kenny Drew, drummer Art Taylor, and alto saxophonist Jackie McLean—all musicians he would later record with. "The first little bands I was involved in during high school were made up of me and my friends trying to play bebop. By that time, Jordan was really part of my roots. It was the early forties, and Charlie Parker's first date as a leader, those Savoy sessions, had been released. That was also Miles Davis' debut—the sessions that included 'Billie's Bounce.' Those sides had a big influence on us." (Cioe 1983, 77)

Even more than the pioneers of bebop, the swing veteran Coleman Hawkins inspired the young saxophonist: "He was the first guy I got involved with listening to closely… He introduced so much harmonic development and movement to the music. His accomplishment was a tremendous challenge and something to strive for." (Cioe 1983, 78) "To me it was a real intellectual experience listening to him." (Berg 1977, 13) And: "In his playing, you could hear the thinking, his studiousness–along with the force and energy." (Cioe 1983, 90)–descriptions, incidentally, that apply as well to Rollins' later playing. It was Hawkins who was responsible for Sonny's change to the tenor saxophone in about 1946. And if we describe the style of the young Rollins, based on his recordings from 1949, as a synthesis of Hawkins' sonority and Parker's linearity, that is really only to single out two of the many influences to which the developing musician was exposed. "I should also say that I was just a horn fan. I dug guys like Lucky Thompson and Lockjaw Davis, who's a really fantastic musician." (Berg 1977, 13). Dexter Gordon, one of the first bop tenorists, also factored in. The synthesis of Hawkins' power, Lester Young's phrasing, and Parker's harmony, which by 1945 Gordon had already achieved, is also evident in Rollins' first records–something which Rollins would readily acknowledge: "No one is original. Everyone is derivative." (Goldberg 1965a, 90)

Saxophonists weren't the only ones who influenced the young Rollins. Two pianists played a crucial role in his development. The first was Bud Powell, who lived on 141st St. "He seemed to have a lot of training and was always practicing and writing... A lot of us used to hang around him, because we looked up to him; he was one of the best players around." (Blancq 1983, 4). It wasn't long before he also got to know the

sonny rollins

with Monk at the Five Spot, 1957

other cult figure of bebop piano. "Eventually I played with Monk. A friend of mine, a guy in our band, was playing with him and asked me to come down to Monk's rehearsal. Then Monk said, 'Well, come and play with me.' So, I used to rehearse at Monk's house with his band which was a very great experience." (Berg 1977, 14) An experience that, like his acquaintance with Powell, involved more than just technique. "One very important thing I learned from Monk was his complete dedication to music. That was his reason for being alive. Nothing else mattered except music, really. I respected that as a kid, I really got that and I said 'Yeah, that's the way it should be.' " Little wonder that, after finishing high school in 1947, there was no question of what direction Rollins would pursue–it had to be a musical career. Rollins joined the Musicians Union, which he could only do by giving his year of birth as 1929–a deliberate misstatement that is still listed in the literature sometimes as fact. With his musician friends (to whom were soon added Fats Navarro, Art Blakey, and other bebop figures), the young tenorist was soon a part of the bebop community. Only in retrospect did Rollins realize how amazing this was. "I don't know how I had the nerve to play with these guys at that time. I had the nerve, I guess, because I did it. But, I wasn't at their level... The fact that they wanted me to play with them also inspired me to keep playing." (Berg 1977, 14) 1949 began promisingly for the 18-year-old professional. In January and April he cut his first sides with the singer Babs Gonzales. In May this led to an offer to record with John Lewis and J.J. Johnson. In August he worked in the studio with his idol Bud Powell, alongside notables Roy Haynes and Fats Navarro.

The downside of these heady associations was exposure to drugs. Inevitably, perhaps, the young Rollins was attracted not only to his heroes' music but to their lifestyle. As early as 1948 he was using and over the course of the next five years heroin would determine the events of his life as much as music. In retrospect, Rollins has interpreted his enthusiasm for bebop and his drug addiction as attempts to escape the pressures of society: "Bebop reflected our alienation from the mainstream," he told Eric Nisenson. "My friends and I believed that bebop was the first musical movement to completely turn away from the minstrel image of most black entertainment... It was more than music–it was a social movement, and we wanted to be part of it." (Nisenson 2000, 28) To be part of the bebop clique thus meant to distance oneself from the crowd, and drugs served the same function. "Using drugs was, in a strange way, a negation of the money ethic. Guys were saying, 'I don't care about this, I don't care how I dress or how I look, all [I] care about is music.' Using drugs was kind of a way for the boppers to express what they thought about American capitalist values." (Nisenson 2000, 38)

1950 started out with good omens. Miles Davis heard Rollins' group perform at the 845 Club in the Bronx. Just 23 at the time, Miles was already a star thanks to his association with Charlie Parker. "After I came down from playing, Miles came up to me and said: 'Look, man, come on and join my band'–just like that, and that was the beginning of a beautiful friendship." (Blancq 1983, 5) Before this friendship could develop, however, addiction put it on hold. Rollins was sentenced to ten months for armed robbery, and so was out of

with Miles, Red Garland, Paul Chambers, and Philly Joe Jones, Randall's Island, 1956 (© Chuck Stewart)

action nearly the whole year. (Rollins used to explain his absence from the New York scene in this period by saying that he had been in Chicago playing with a "legendary" drummer named Ike Day—this Ike Day is not documented on record.) So Rollins' first recordings with Davis were put off until January of 1951. Davis made a good report of the tenorist to Prestige producer Bob Weinstock, leading in turn to Rollins' first recordings under his own name the following December. In general Davis seems to have been more a musical than a personal influence on Rollins' during his early professional years. "Miles was the guy that brought me out of my shell in certain ways. I felt that I couldn't really play as well as certain other guys that were big at that time and Miles said, 'No man, you can do it. That's why I have you in my band instead of some other guys.' So he spurred me and pushed me a lot of times." (Berg 1977, 14)

Whoever wants a vivid impression of the scene for young musicians in New York in the early fifties is referred to the relevant chapters in Miles Davis' autobiography. There you will learn that much of Davis and Rollins' time was occupied with finding drugs, and hanging out in bars, pool halls, and nightclubs. In Davis' words: "I was really heavy into heroin and also began to hang out with Sonny Rollins and his Sugar Hill Harlem crowd. This group included, besides Sonny, the pianist Gil Coggins, Jackie McLean, Walter Bishop, Art Blakey..., Art Taylor and Max Roach ... People loved Sonny Rollins up in Harlem and everywhere else. He was a legend, almost a god to a lot of the younger musicians... I had a job at the Audubon Ballroom and so I asked Sonny to join the band,

and he did. Coltrane was in that band, as was Art Blakey on drums. All of them–Sonny, Art, and Coltrane–were using a lot of heroin at the time, so being around them a lot like I was just got me into it deeper." (Davis 1989, 123ff.)

His heroin habit explains not only the many musical shifts and changes in Rollins' recordings from this period, but also the erratic course of his career until 1955. Miscellaneous stays in hospital rehab wards, and a second jail sentence (1952–1953) waylaid the career that had begun so full of promise. In 1952 Rollins made no recordings at all, and the following year was only slightly more productive. But one session from this year–with Miles Davis and Charlie Parker (on tenor)–was of great significance for Rollins, and not mainly for musical reasons: "A lot of things I was doing because I figured they were the things to be done because a lot of my idols did them. But Bird never encouraged me to do anything that would prove wrong for myself. And on that record date, he really told me what to do so far as music and my life were concerned." (Goldberg 1965a, 93) To be precise: "I told Bird I was clean and I wasn't... When I saw his reaction–he was beaming and happy–it struck me about what this meant to him. I realized I would have to stop. I said: 'I'm really going to show Bird I understood what he meant.' " (West 1974, 23) But there was a considerable lag between this good intention and its fulfillment. Only toward the end of 1954, nearly two years after the session with Parker, and after making additional recordings with Davis, Monk, and under his own name, did Rollins enroll himself in a four-and-a-half-month detox program in the US Public Health Service Hospital of Lexington KY. When he

was released in the spring of 1955, Parker had already died.

the "new bird" (1955–1959)

"I overcame [the addiction] because I had something else to put my time and energy into, which in my case was music." (Jarrett 1990, 8) After leaving the clinic, Rollins was smart enough not to immerse himself again in the temptations of the nightclub scene. "This was a period in which I had to prove myself. I wasn't quite ready to get back into the music scene." (West 1974, 23) Instead he went to Chicago, rented a small room in the YMCA, practiced at night, and worked as a custodian during the day. "My job was at a small office and factory, and I would sweep out, and mop the floors, and clean the toilets. I did it very well, and conscientiously, and I enjoyed it for a while. When I left, my employer was very sorry to see me go." (Goldberg 1965a, 93f.) His next job was equally non-artistic–loading trucks–a job he took because he liked physical labor.

When Rollins returned to jazz having been absent a good year, it was less a conscious decision than the result of happy chance. In November 1955 the Max Roach–Clifford Brown quintet, one of the most renowned combos of the time, made a guest spot at the Bee Hive, one of the typical neighborhood bars on Chicago's South Side. And because Harold Land had returned to his native California, where his wife was expecting, the band needed a saxophone player. They asked Rollins, whom Roach already knew from some recordings they had made together with J.J. Johnson in 1949, whether he would fill in—which he did so ably (the results can be heard on the double LP *Live at the Bee Hive*) that Roach asked him to join the band on a permanent basis. That month Rollins returned to New York as a full-fledged member.

The eighteen months that Rollins played in Roach's combo mark his breakthrough to the undisputed young star on tenor, the premier saxophonist of hard bop. Up to then, Rollins had been a musicians' musician, a colleague esteemed in professional circles but little known to the jazz audience at large; his first recordings on Prestige, then a small label, had done little to change that. And criticism in the trades had not all been favorable. In his review in *Down Beat* of the October 1954 recordings with Thelonious Monk, Nat Hentoff, reacting to Ira Gitler's complaint on the album's liner notes that critics were deaf to Rollins' virtues, wrote: "Ira Gitler's argumentative notes fail to convince me that Rollins possesses particularly 'individual ideas' or that his blowing is 'tremendous.' Rollins swings hard, and he plays with considerable warmth, but as has been stated here before, he lacks freshness of conception and his imagination is not individually distinctive enough to raise him to the top level of jazz improvisers."

But Rollins' first record after his comeback—the LP *Worktime*, recorded in December 1955 with the rhythm section of the Roach–Brown quintet—revealed a player of such obvious authority, inventiveness, and virtuosity, that even skeptics were won over. Nat Hentoff sang quite a different tune in the May 2 1956 *Down Beat*: "Rhythmically, no tenor today swings any more authoritatively than Sonny and few are as sustainedly

with Clifford Brown at Basin Street NYC, 1956
(© Chuck Stewart)

driven as he. His ideas erupt from the horn with bullet-like propulsion. Melodically, his conception is angular, and his lines are heatedly jagged rather than softly flowing. His tone also is hard, though not harsh. Rollins is close to nonpareil at the kind of playing he obviously prefers."

Many appearances across the country ensued with the Roach–Brown quintet, along with a rapid series of record releases—with Miles, Roach (these on the renowned EmArcy label), as well as under his own name. Within a short time, Rollins was no longer a "musicians' musician," but a household name among jazz fans. The jazz public, looking for the next hero after Parker, could well believe that in the person of this young tenor saxophonist they had found the 'new Bird'—a tag especially current following the release of the LPs *Tenor Madness* and *Saxophone Colossus* (recorded in May and June, respectively, of 1956). *Saxophone Colossus* was treated to a famous and influential analysis by Gunther Schuller in 1958, and Whitney Balliett, writing in the *New Yorker*, said that it revealed Rollins as "possibly the most incisive and influential jazz instrumentalist since Charlie Parker," with a "tumultuous and brilliant imagination that probably equals Parker's." (Goldberg 1965a, 97)

The high level of quality that characterizes Rollins' recordings between November 1955 and June 1956 is due not just to Max Roach and Clifford Brown's musical inspiration, but to Sonny's new-found equilibrium in body and soul after years of physical and emotional turmoil. Clifford Brown, in particular, served as a role model in this respect: "Clifford was a profound influence on my personal life. He showed me that it was possible to live a good, clean life, and still be a good jazz musician." (Goldberg 1965a, 94) "Clifford was a fantastic person and musician, just an angel. There was nothing he would do that would make you mad. His demeanor and temperament were so straight and even. Anyway, as a person as well as a musician, Clifford had a tremendous influence on me. I was kind of wild when I first went in the band, in an emotional way. But Clifford was so together as a person you wouldn't have believed it. For a guy that plays so much to be so humble and beautiful, it was just amazing. So I tried to be nice after that." (Berg 1977, 14) The musical and human empathy between the two musicians was cut short when Clifford Brown died in an auto accident on June 26, 1956; the two other people in the car, Richard Powell and his wife Nancy, were also killed. In subsequent months trumpeter Donald Byrd and Kenny Dorham, as well as pianists Wade Legge, Ray Bryant, and Billy Wallace, would replace them. The musical as well as personal loss was irreparable, however.

Meanwhile, the young star on saxophone had become so popular that his commercial value soared. And so toward the end of 1956 he ended his exclusive contract with Prestige and until 1959 adopted the more lucrative role of independent musician. Every jazz label of note at the time seems to have wanted a Rollins LP in their catalog–and got one. Recordings for Blue Note, Contemporary, Riverside, Period, Verve, and MetroJazz followed in swift succession. While many are successful, some are just routine–that was inevitable, and Rollins seemed aware of it. In interviews from this period he expresses dissatisfaction with his own playing, as well as anxiety about losing his own style because of the 'new Bird' label–about listening to the enthusiastic critics instead of his own self-critical inner voice.

In this period Rollins made his first trip to the West Coast with the Max Roach Quintet. Some significant meetings took place there: he was introduced to Ornette Coleman and Don Cherry, the pioneers of Free Jazz, at that time still unknown beyond the local scene (where Coleman was more notorious than famous). Rollins jammed with them, not in public, but privately by the Pacific shore. And on the morning of March 7, 1957–3am, to be exact, owing to prior engagements of the musicians–he made his first trio recording with Ray Brown and Shelly Manne. Apart from Gerry Mulligan's pioneering ensembles, the piano was still *de rigueur*, but over the next two years the pianoless trio would become one of Rollins' favorite settings. Rollins also got married for the first time–to a dancer named Dawn Finney (some sources give her name as Dawn Adams). The marriage would last only a short time, and Rollins has said little–and that reluctantly–about it since then: "I just wanted to get married. So I looked around, and found somebody, and I did it." (Goldberg 1965a, 98)

Only now–and with hesitation–did Rollins yield to the public expectation to finally lead his own ensemble. In May 1957, he left the Max Roach Quintet to briefly rejoin Miles Davis, who was in need of a saxophonist since John Coltrane had been sacked. In late October, though, at the Village Vanguard, he presented for the first time his own working group–a quintet with trumpeter Donald Byrd. But this was anything but a tight-knit group under Rollins' direction. Byrd remained with the band only a week, while pianists came and went almost every day, until at last only a trio consisting of sax, bass, and drums remained. Even then the personnel would change–sometimes during the same night. So on the legendary November 3rd *A Night at the Village Vanguard* recordings you can hear, in turn, bassists Donald Bailey and Wilbur Ware, as well as drummers Pete LaRoca and Elvin Jones. And it was an entirely different trio–with Oscar Pettiford and Max Roach–that performed the landmark *Freedom Suite* in February and March the following year. (More about this musical as well as sociological landmark will be found in the second section about Rollins' personality, as well as in the stylistic chapter.)

Although the acclaimed new star had no trouble booking appearances and studio sessions, he was not entirely comfortable in the new leadership role. The extra-musical duties that came with the job took energy away from the music itself. And he felt that his return to the club scene involved him in a treadmill that kept him from those goals he had set when he first got out. As early as the spring of 1957 he told Contemporary producer Lester Koenig that he intended to "withdraw from the nightclub scene, find a place to settle, study, and work for my bachelor's degree in music." (liner notes to *Way Out West*) A year later, in a *Down Beat* interview from July 1958, he told of a depression that overcame him after an unsatisfying live date, and said: "Right now, I feel I just want to get away for awhile. I think I need a lot of things. One of them is time–time to study and finish some things I started a long time ago. I think if I could go to Europe, or even get away from the New York scene for awhile, I could assess things, judge myself more objectively. Being a leader takes up a lot of time. Most of the time I'm working on band business when I should be working on the music. I never seem to have time to work, practice, and write. Everything becomes secondary to going to work every night, and wondering how the band sounds and whether our appearances are okay. Part of this, I think, started when I went with Max [Roach] and [Clifford] Brown. I only wanted to fill in awhile. I found out I was staying on. I lost the thread of a lot of things I had planned to do." (Cerulli 1958, 16)

In retrospect, his statement anticipates the much-discussed sabbatical Rollins would take between 1959 and 1961. At the time, however, it could be interpreted merely as the testiness of an overworked artist. The concerts were numerous (in the autumn of 1958, for instance, he participated in the nationwide "Jazz for Moderns" tour organized by promoter Ed Sarkesian). So were the festival appearances (in October he appeared at the first Monterey Jazz Festival), and club dates (he guested at York's Five Spot in November, but broke the engagement off after a week because Charles Mingus, who alternated nights with him, treated him horribly (Priestley 1982, 107)). Until the autumn of 1958 there was a dense schedule of recording dates too, concluding with the Contemporary recordings in October. In February and March 1959 there followed an extremely successful tour of Europe, documented on record, that took the Rollins trio—now with the brilliant young bass–drums duo of Henry Grimes and Pete LaRoca—to Spain, Italy, Denmark, Sweden, England, Belgium, and France. "I've come to Europe to get a chance to get hold of myself and expand my knowledge," explained Rollins to a Swedish interviewer on March 1 (liner notes to *St. Thomas*). Back in the States there was another two-week engagement at the Five Spot with his old friend and mentor Thelonious Monk.

But then in August 1959 Rollins announced he was withdrawing from the jazz scene—indefinitely.

years of searching (1959–1971)

That a jazz soloist at the height of critical and commercial success should simply disappear from public was unprecedented in the New York of 1959. Rumors were rampant in the jazz world over the next twenty-seven months—had Rollins retired because he felt overshadowed by his supposed rival John Coltrane? Had he gone into seclusion to come to grips with the musical challenge of the *new thing* represented by Ornette Coleman and Cecil Taylor?

Dissatisfaction with his music was certainly behind Rollins' decision—dissatisfaction, however, not when compared with others, but compared with the success and journalistic acclaim his own playing earned. "Despite what's been written about me, I don't think I've played as well as I'm able," he told *Down Beat* journalist Joe Goldberg in 1961. "I've only done a small part of what I want to do and I felt that the first thing I had to do was get myself together." (Goldberg 1965a, 103) And, as he explained, this involved more than music. The failed first marriage made him address his excessive alcohol and nicotine intake (even after he kicked heroin, dependency continue to be a problem in his life in one form or another). So he imposed a rigorous fitness program on himself and quit smoking and drinking. And only a month after his comeback, in September 1959, he got married again. "I've read several studies which prove that people who have had an unhappy first marriage are much more likely to be happy in their second one. You know more and your feet are on the ground. It seems to have worked out for me." (Goldberg 1965a, 103)

How did Rollins live during the 2 + years of isolation? With his second wife Lucille, he occupied a small apartment on Grand Street in Manhattan's Lower East Side–without a telephone, in order to keep the world at bay. He broadened his knowledge of music theory by studying piano, as well as harmony and counterpoint. At first he practiced the saxophone at home, "But I was very loud. There was a girl next door who was having a baby, and I was anxious to see if my playing would give that baby bad ears... Then I discovered the Williamsburg Bridge, which is near where I live, and I stopped practicing at home. I started walking over the bridge, and I found out it's a superb place to practice. Night or day. You're up over the whole world. You can look down on the whole scene. There is the skyline, the water, the harbor... You can blow as loud as you want. It makes you think. The grandeur gives you perspective. And people never bother you." (Russell 1961, 42) No one bothered him at first, anyway. But when journalist Ralph Berton discovered Rollins practicing alone, and wrote a lightly fictionalized story that appeared in the *New Yorker,* Rollins' tranquility came to an end. Colleagues, jazz fans and journalists were curious: What did Rollins practice, how had his playing changed? The soprano saxophonist Steve Lacy, whom Rollins invited to his *al fresco* practice sessions, reported: "It's very hard to get a sound there, with the wind whipping by, so if you can play well there it would be the simplest thing in the world to play in a club. We don't have any particular material that we're rehearsing, just whatever comes to mind. We're just trying to find out about ourselves musically. We practice fingering, intonation, tone, scales, intervals, everything. I've never seen anyone in love with the tenor saxophone the way Sonny is... He knows everything about it." (Goldberg 1965a, 106) Rollins himself says: "When I quit working, I tried to revise the way I played the horn. Completely. But then I amended that. Instead, I made an exploration of the horn." (Russell 1961, 42) In the June 9 1960 *Down Beat* Rollins published a notice intended to reassure his fans and lay the rumors to rest. "I am at present engaged in numerous pursuits, the most pressing of which are my writing and composing. These endeavors are demanding of the greater portion of my time, concentration, and energies. They will be best brought to fruition by my maintaining a certain amount of seclusion and divorcing myself as much as possible from my professional career during this period."

To be sure, Rollins didn't lead the life of a hermit. He kept in touch with colleagues like Coltrane, Coleman, and Lacy, and occasionally visited jazz clubs to stay abreast of recent developments–especially Coleman's innovations. He took courses in philosophy, and became a member of the Rosicrucian sect. Royalties from the many recordings he made in the early years, a generous advance from the copyright society BMI, and the salary of his wife Lucille, who had a good job as an executive secretary, kept financial worries in the background. But the media racket about the jazz recluse of Grand Street, the lonesome saxophonist high above the East River, finally became too much. And unforeseen and costly dental problems upset his financial equilibrium. So–as in 1955– Rollins' return to the scene came earlier than he had planned. "I hadn't really intended to come out yet. I wasn't quite ready to come back." (Berg 1977, 38)

Expectations were naturally high–too high, as it turned out–when Rollins premiered his new quartet at the Jazz Gallery in November '61. The quartet included guitarist Jim Hall, bassist Bob Cranshaw, and (briefly) drummer Walter Perkins. The public as well as the press gave him an enthusiastic reception; and yet in the journalistic ovations one sometimes caught a note of disappointment that the musical dividend from the twenty-seven month layoff wasn't larger. The radically new Rollins that some had hoped for, others feared, did not–at least for now–show up. And *The Bridge*, the first LP he released after the comeback (produced January–February 1962) offered new ideas, to be sure, but no grand new conception. The unusually lucrative deal he had struck with major label RCA–$90,000 for five LPs over two years–gives a fair indication, though, of how much the media buzz over the sequestered saxophonist had boosted his market value.

With Rollins' second release on RCA–*What's New?*–it might appear to the casual fan, attending more to the promotional copy on the cover than to the music on disk, that the saxophonist was following the new bossa nova fad, rather than adding his own accents. His collaboration with Ornette Coleman associates Don Cherry and Billy Higgins, however, showed his readiness to face the challenges posed by the avant-garde; this partnership lasted from the summer of 1962 until spring of the following year. And unlike Coltrane, whose first contact with the Coleman circle (documented on the album *The Avant-Garde*) was rather disappointing, Rollins adapted very well to the new formal and harmonic openness of their interplay. He did not try to copy Coleman, but adopted his flexibility for his own purposes. A tour of Europe with Cherry, Higgins, and bass player Henry Grimes led to a meeting with another pioneer of free jazz. In Denmark he met saxophone renegade Albert Ayler, who was working on a radical new approach of pure sound-playing, "escaping notes to sound," as Ayler put it. Rollins' praise of Ayler was more than lip service as his own experiments with sound during this period demonstrate (experiments that would try the patience of devotees of the classic Rollins tone). More costly tooth treatments after the return from Europe forced another hiatus of some months (not for the last time in his career).

Rollins' musical activities in the following years could be described as erratic. Progressive recordings, marked by sonic and structural freedom, alternate with comparatively conventional ones; collaborations (sporadically documented on record) with young avant-gardists like Don Cherry, David Izenzon, Charles Moffett, Rashied Ali, and Paul Bley, stand alongside releases with mainstream musicians such as Ray Bryant and Tommy Flanagan—or veterans like Coleman Hawkins. His public appearances were just as unpredictable. In general, however, Sonny Rollins in the sixties was one of the few musicians of his generation who managed to bridge the gap between bebop and free jazz—always interested in what's new, without denying his roots or the jazz tradition. If Rollins' search yielded less dramatic results than his friends Miles Davis or John Coltrane, the fact that he hardly ever found himself in a stable lineup is no doubt partly to blame. The eight months he spent with Cherry and Higgins represented, for him, an unusual degree of stability. Afterwards, practically every Rollins appearance, every new record, introduced a new group of musicians.

At the end of 1963 Rollins toured Japan with Paul Bley, Henry Grimes, drummer Roy McCurdy, and trumpeter Reshid Kmal. This was Rollins' first trip to the Far East, and marked his first substantial contact with Eastern thought. A Japanese jazz fan introduced the saxophonist to a Zen master, with whom he kept in contact during the following years personally and by letter. To this same period belongs his first intense exposure to the techniques of yoga, which would finally take the place of the body-building exercises he had ceaselessly, even religiously, practiced up to then (and which he had even tried to get the chronically overweight Charles Mingus to participate in). The founding of a "Sonny Rollins Yoga for Americans" club showed (again) that Rollins was keen to share his personal discoveries with others.

At the time, one might have looked upon Rollins' involvement with eastern philosophies and physical regimes as exotic hobbies, or—as in the case of Hatha yoga—as practical tools for a musician who depended on his physical fitness to perform. But in the following years they undoubtedly acquired deeper personal significance. In order to understand why, one should consider how Rollins' situation changed in the latter half of the sixties. About 1965, he was in an enviable position: he had a record contract with a big company, steady offers of lucrative club and festival appearances (such as the Jazzfest Berlin in 1965, or in March 1966 a "Titans of the Tenor Concert" in New York's Philharmonic Hall with Coltrane and Coleman Hawkins)–even offers from the affluent film industry (the score to *Alfie,* 1966). Just two years later, things looked very different. The contract with Impulse, signed in 1965, was not renewed, owing to Rollins' dissatisfaction with the artistic and financial conditions. Appearances at his asking price, to which he believed he was entitled owing to his stature, became less frequent. ("If they want Sonny Rollins, then they have to pay my price. If I don't get it now, when am I going to get it?" (Gitler 1969, 19)) The popularity of rock completely dislocated the world of the jazz clubs, jazz festivals, and jazz record companies. There were small but no less nagging personal problems: chronic tooth difficulties owing to a rigid embouchure, and the physiological as well as psychological consequences of a reckless use of drugs ("I had a weight problem and was using a lot of pills–amphetamines. I was very paranoid. I wasn't getting much done. I was doing things, but I wasn't going anywhere." (West 1974, 21)

Under these circumstances, the second Japanese tour of January–February 1968 appears as the culmination of a geographical and spiritual odyssey. After the concerts, Rollins deepened his Zen studies in Mishima, at the foot of Mt. Fuji, under the direction of the Zen master Oki, whom he had met five years earlier. Then he continued on to India, where for five months he studied meditation and Vedic philosophy with

Swami Chinmayananda in the Ashram Sandipani Sadhanalaya at Powaai-See near Bombay. (He also performed his first solo concert there for the benefit of his fellow ashram residents.)

It was a while, however, before Rollins could harvest the fruits of these efforts. For the time being, they remained elusive. "When I came back from India, I was very serene and peaceful. But this tranquility only lasted a couple of weeks before I gradually began to come down." (West 1974, 21f.) And it was not just the business; on a human level, in his interactions with other musicians, he had increasingly unpleasant experiences. "I had gotten fed up with the music scene and fighting with musicians to get them to try to play my music." (Fiofori 1971, 14) There was another tour of Europe in September 1968, including a concert in Denmark with Mary Lou Williams; less frequent, seldom wholly satisfying guest spots in American clubs with rapidly shifting personnel. Then, after appearances on the West Coast in September 1969, a breaking point was reached. "I had had it… I didn't want to play, I didn't want to hear music and I didn't want to know about music or anything. I was very, very upset because that was the first time I had gotten to the point where actually I didn't even want to know about music." (Fiofori 1971, 14) For twenty-one months up until June of 1971–for the longest stretch of his career–Sonny again fell silent.

self-realization (1971–2001)

The career of Sonny Rollins can be divided along the self-imposed breaks. The first years as a professional lead to the

sabbatical of 1954–55; the years he rose to become the Star of Hard Bop are succeeded by the Bridge interlude; the period of musical and spiritual searching is followed by period of total musical abstinence that lasted from September 1969 until June 1971. Since then–i.e., for three decades now–Rollins has remained active on the jazz scene without significant interruption. He concertizes regularly (if not as often as he once did), and just as dependably releases an album every year or (more recently) two. He leads a life devoid of the scandal that vaults other jazzmen into the headlines. "Unspectacular" may be the best word to characterize his musical as well as his personal activities since 1971. And if that disappoints scandal mongers and fashion hounds, it nevertheless proves that Rollins finally achieved the artistic and personal balance he had sought for a very long time–balance between periods of touring, concertizing, recording in the studio–and periods of renewal, rest, practice, and meditation.

"I realized that it is a special, a holy gift to be able to make music, and that it would be wrong in a religious sense not to use it." (Endress 1977, 7) This realization of his mission as a musician–a mission in the genuinely spiritual sense–enabled Rollins to return to making of music. In June 1971 he appeared at a jazz festival in the Norwegian city of Kongsberg with a Scandinavian rhythm section (Bobo Stenson, piano; Arild Andersen, bass; Jon Christensen, drums). Some months passed before the official comeback in the jazz capital of New York. With pianist Al Dailey, bassist Larry Ridley, and drummer David Lee, Rollins undertook a one-week engagement at the Village Vanguard, which drew record crowds to the club.

opposite: Sonny in 1974
(© Jan Persson)

Owner Max Gordon immediately hired the group for another run in April. Fans of the 'old' Sonny Rollins of the late fifties could breathe a sigh of relief: Rollins classics like "St. Thomas," and standards like "Three Little Words," "There Is No Greater Love," and "In A Sentimental Mood" set the keynote.

That Rollins in the months of retreat had undergone not just a personal but also a musical metamorphosis, that there was more to the 'new' Rollins than just nostalgia, became clear on the first album for Milestone, recorded in July 1972 after an absence of six years from the studio. Here, on the dryly-named *Next Album*, you could hear not only Rollins' incorporation of contemporary rock rhythms, but his debut on soprano saxophone. Asked why he took up the instrument, he said candidly—"Coltrane. He really brought everything together for the soprano. He put it into the limelight. I still get a lot from John. I feel that, at one point, he got a lot from me, and now I'm catching up with him." (Porter 1974, 15) And while the soprano sax remained just an episode in his music (in this respect like his experimentation with the lyricon, a synthesizer for woodwind players), fusion-oriented numbers as well as cover versions of pop hits would continue to feature on his records and in his concerts.

As with Miles Davis, Rollins' audience was divided between traditionalists and supporters of the new direction. The latter, to judge by the critical consensus, were in the minority. Judgments like the following, from a review of a Rollins' concert that appeared in *Down Beat* in 1977, expressed what many Rollins' fans felt, if few put it so bluntly: "One of the most depressing trends of the 70's has been certain great jazz musicians' embrace of unchallenging music that leads them to play far below their capabilities. Sonny Rollins is now one of those musicians... Rollins' new repertoire consists mostly of banal funk and West Indian-flavored tunes, and there is little in this new music to inspire any creative improviser... As a result, Rollins... sounded strained on this 'contemporary' material. Worse still, he turned in mediocre solos even on the new jazz originals in his book. (Significantly, most of those tunes were nothing to write home about, either.) On the straight-ahead material, Rollins alternated between paraphrasing the rhythmic characteristics of the pieces and echoing some of the most shopworn phrases in John Coltrane's 'sheets of sound' vocabulary. And remember that magnificent, tubular Rollins tone? In its place, Rollins substituted a grating timbre reminiscent of Gato Barbieri's. While I'm not a Barbieri fan, I accept the premise that the Argentinian's sound is an integral part of his style. Coming from Sonny, though, this sound was an affectation and an anemic one at that ... Rollins' rhythm section [Mike Wolff, piano; Aurell Ray, guitar; Don Pate, electric bass; Eddie Moore, drums], whose chief attribute was loudness, met the limited demands of most of the music ... Oh, well–perhaps Frank Zappa is right. Maybe jazz musicians will forget how to improvise and will get really good at playing disco music." (Kirchner 1977, 37)

Other critics clothed their reservations in more courteous phrases, or, more often, let them be read only between the lines of their generally favorable reports about the jazz giant come back to life. Only years later, with the release of albums like *Sunny Days, Starry Nights* and the *Solo Album* would he completely succeed in gratifying long-deferred expectations for the 'new Rollins.'

He certainly did not lack for public acknowledgment after the comeback. He was awarded a $10,000 Guggenheim grant in 1972 to support work on a concert for tenor saxophone and orchestra, a project that he had envisaged as early as the fifties but only brought to realization in 1986. (Four other jazz musicians–Carla Bley, Keith Jarrett, Mary Lou Williams, and George Russell–also received Guggenheims that year, which was remarkable in that there had only been one jazz figure among the previous fifteen recipients.) Two years later, in 1974, he was inducted into *Down Beat*'s Hall of Fame, the pantheon of jazz figures alive or dead–the thirty-eighth to be so honored. Even the popular media, usually indifferent to less popular forms of improvised music, now lionized the living legend. In 1979 Rollins appeared on the Tonight Show, where he performed an unaccompanied tenor solo. An appearance at the White House (with McCoy Tyner, Ron Carter, and Max Roach) in June 1978 represented some kind of official acknowledgment by the political powers that be. In general he focused his concertizing on well-paid tours of Europe and Japan, with the occasional guest appearance on American campuses or in larger clubs like New York's Bottom Line or The Great American Music Hall in San Francisco. These bursts of public activity alternated with long periods of regeneration on his farm in Germantown in upstate New York, which has been his permanent home since the mid-seventies. An apartment in New York's Tribeca district functions mainly as a place of business, and since 1972 is run by his wife Lucille. It is Lucille Rollins also who in 1981, together with Sonny, took over the job of producing his records at Milestone, a job formerly held by Orrin Keepnews. Why has Rollins remained faithful to the comparatively small Milestone label, despite numerous lucrative offers from outside? "I've been with them a long time, and they don't press me about what to do. Which is the reason I'm with them. I've had the chance to go with Columbia and some other companies with better publicity and distribution. But I can be here and not dictated to." (Cook 1985, 30)

Only rarely since 1971 has Rollins given up or shared the leader's role. In 1978 his label persuaded him to participate in a nation-wide tour (documented on record) with the "Milestone Jazzstars" (Rollins, McCoy Tyner, Ron Carter, Al Foster). In 1981 he turned up as guest soloist on the Rolling Stones album *Tattoo You,* and that same year engaged in a public tenor duel with Grover Washington, Jr., and went on an All-Star tour of Japan with George Duke, Stanley Clarke, and Al Foster. "It's not ideal, but people like to see people like this together, so you have to go along with it... You very often feel unfulfilled." (Blumenthal 1982, 17) A combination of commercial considerations and genuine interest in supporting young musicians has induced him, now and then, to invite them on stage with him as "special guest stars." In April 1983 he performed in New York's Town Hall with Wynton Marsalis (a concert he had to break off, however, when he suffered a bout of dizziness). That summer he toured Japan with Pat Metheny, and in 1989 Wynton's brother Branford had the honor of playing alongside his idol in Weil Hall, leading to a recording together later that year.

Prior to that, however, Rollins realized two ambitions that he had alluded to as early as 1958 in an interview with *Down Beat.* In 1985 he gave his first extended concert as unaccompanied soloist in the sculpture garden of New York's Museum of Modern Art; the following year, in Japan, the Concerto for B flat Tenor Saxophone and Symphony Orchestra finally saw the light of day. This remarkable, if not altogether successful, example of his involvement with the symphonic tradition of the Old World can as yet only be heard on the soundtrack to the film *Saxophone Colossus,* which Robert Mugge directed in 1986. The film, incidentally, entails painful memories for Rollins: during the filming of the concert (released on LP/CD as *G-Man*) he fell off the stage and broke his foot. According to an interview in *Down Beat,* he has never been able to bring himself to view the movie to the (bitter) end. (Kalbacher 1977, 18)

In Rollins' career in the eighties and nineties there has been little of the ups and downs that marked the fifties and sixties–no sabbaticals, no comebacks, no sudden stylistic shifts. To the casual fan he might appear complacent, enjoying his position as a jazz elder statesman who has the privilege of making his own decisions about his career–when, where, and under what financial conditions to perform, who to play with, what to record. Yet this would be a fairly superficial view. True, Rollins has found his place in the world and in the jazz scene, his modus operandi, and has gained a measure of peace. But Rollins the perfectionist is not one to rest on his laurels. His constant quest for self-expression, for the free flow of

in Copenhagen, 1968
(© Jan Persson)

biography

musical ideas, keeps him on his toes. But, this is, for the most part, a private activity. There is little in his life to make headlines; instead, there is an undemanding schedule of appearances at major festivals and in concert halls at home and abroad ("Jazz needs some dignity. It needs to be looked at as a serious, important art form. And if you're going to be playing in nightclubs, I don't care what you say, you're not going to get that respect for it" (Belden 1997, 25)). There is a small-group recording once every two years for the Milestone label, invariably with a familiar blend of jazz and calypso originals, and one or two Broadway or film classics. In short: nothing much to satisfy the appetite of journalists on the lookout for "events," "trends," or sensational details from an artist's private life. The fact that there should be an improviser solitarily working on his craft with great patience, rigor, and dedication, preferring the familiar context of a small group of highly competent, if not trend-setting musicians, is not very compatible with the world of "jazz news" and "charts." What's more, Rollins, the recluse, is not one to seek the critic's attention or to flatter their tastes. As he told Eric Nisenson: "Fortunately, the role of the jazz critic is not as crucial as it used to be. When I started out, the critics for *Down Beat* or *Metronome* had a disproportionate effect on your ability to get work. They could kill you. But now it doesn't really make any difference. I tell them all to go to hell, in my way, because I don't care." (Nisenson 2000, 195)

This is pretty aggressive language for somebody who doesn't care. In fact, Rollins' rare public statements make it clear that he *does* care what's being written about him—and that he is

Sonny at 70
(courtesy fantasy records)

hurt especially by record reviews that habitually praise his playing while putting down the efforts of his sidemen. (In the words of Jim Macnie, reviewing Rollins' CD *Global Warming* in the July 1998 issue of *Down Beat*: "...Everyone in the band isn't Sonny Rollins. When the boss strolls, the inspiration flags and the energy drops."). So when *Down Beat* author John McDonough approached Rollins for an interview in 1992, the first question was: "Is this going to be another negative, punch-Sonny-Rollins-in-the-eye article for *Down Beat*?" (McDonough 2000, 22) These are not the words of someone indifferent to the critical commentary his music generates. Rollins, the song musician *extraordinaire*, needs partners familiar with the incredible archive of tunes in his head. "With a lot of these younger guys I have to bring in the [sheet music of the] tunes and show it to them. If I want to play, say, 'Dancing in the Dark,' a lot of these kids have not even heard that song. Sometimes that is hard, because just seeing the chord changes may not be enough for them to feel comfortable playing a certain tune." (Nisenson 2000, 207). So allowances must be made for the gap in knowledge between the master and the younger generation he associates with. Still, critics may be pardoned for hoping for the much talked-about Max Roach–Sonny Rollins reunion, eagerly expecting the second Sonny Rollins solo album, or patiently awaiting the long-promised recording of his concerto for saxophone and orchestra. Or for dreaming about collaborations with vintage free spirits and expert song players like Paul Bley, Paul Motian, and Gary Peacock...

"He's a slow, deliberate talker, one who'll circle around a topic for a while, repeating himself as he does..., ready to chew over any question raised for as long as it takes him to explore it—which, come to think of it, is a lot like the way he improvises." Kevin Whitehead's description of Sonny Rollins the interviewee is the most concise description of Rollins' speech known to me—and may offer another explanation why Rollins rarely makes headlines. Sonny Rollins is not one to make rash judgements on a fellow musician—or any other human being, for that matter. His moral commitment not to hurt anyone's feelings, not to be unfair to anyone, results in carefully worded statements that require a certain ability to read between the lines.

So what can we know about Sonny Rollins, the man? That he is an avid reader, especially on spiritual and political topics. That he is deeply concerned about the ecological state of the planet (a concern reflected in the title of his CD *Global Warming*), and espouses an "anti-technological" philosophy. That, although usually tolerant of all kinds of music, he does not share Max Roach's view that hip-hop is the bebop of today, but feels that, while valuable as a means of social comment, hip-hop can in no way compare with bebop for intellectual depth (he has declined several invitations to collaborate with rap artists). That he appreciates the work of young jazz musicians like Kenny Garrett and James Carter (two highly rhythmic saxophonists, like Rollins himself), but spends little time actually listening to music, preferring to spend time watching film classics like *The Blue Angel*, *The Sky's the Limit*, and *The Maltese Falcon*.

What can we expect from Rollins in the future? The concerts and recordings of recent years bear witness to musical consolidation of a high order, of a stylistic eclecticism with Rollins' unmistakable stamp–along with bursts of improvisational energy that, despite the usually predictable musical framework, never give rise to a feeling of routine. Rollins himself keeps all his options open and will only commit to one thing: "I'm looking forward to putting more air in my horn."

personality—
the doubtful giant

In his liner notes to the groundbreaking album *Saxophone Colossus* (1956) Ira Gitler reflects on the title's connotations. "Colossus"—the name derives from the Colossus of Rhodes, one of the Seven Wonders of the Ancient World: a hundred-foot-tall bronze statue of Apollo erected c. 280 BC, which came toppling down in an earthquake in 224 BC. Rollins though, is certainly proof against any such disaster. "His contributions to jazz are of a nature that places them above destruction by earthquakes or any other natural phenomena."

As far as Rollins' place in jazz history is concerned, one has to credit Gitler's powers of prescience, forty-five years after the fact. But where Rollins the man is concerned, the historical analogy with the tottering giant is more appropriate than Gitler could have supposed. Because this is just the puzzling but fascinating paradox about Theodore Walter Rollins: his acknowledged greatness as a trend-setting musician goes hand in hand with an apparent insecurity and vacillation in musical as well as personal matters.

the erratic sonny rollins

"Excellence seldom goes hand in hand with consistency"—so begins Joe Goldberg in the liner notes to the album *Newk's Time.* The theme runs like a red thread throughout the literature on Rollins. Ever since the fifties, inconsistency is the reproach leveled at Rollins' live performances as well as his recordings. Dick Hadlock complained of "musical confusion" and "the agony of fragmentary ideas" after an appearance at San Francisco's Jazz Workshop in the fall of '58 (Hadlock 1958). Others put it less harshly; but that there are inconsistencies in Rollins' music—within his improvisations, among various pieces, between different appearances and recordings—this is a persistent refrain in Rollins criticism. And the charge of being erratic extends beyond the music. Rollins has also been unpredictable in his onstage behavior, his outward appearance, his behavior toward his fellow musicians. Goldberg's cynical remark about "one of his favorite hobbies, firing drummers" indicates that, depending on his moods, Rollins could be a capricious leader. What he wanted musically was difficult to predict ahead of time—for the public, for his sidemen, maybe even for himself. And so the supreme command he gives his sidemen was, and is: Expect the unexpected. (Berg 1977, 39)

There has been a lot of speculation about Rollins' psychology and the source of his volatility. What compels an artist, who has reached the highest musical level, to venture into new terrain over and over, be the terrain ever so slippery? Perfectionism, relentless self-criticism—that is one answer, and the one he favors. "One of my indulgences is a quest for perfection, and this can go on and on forever." Or: "I can say that I've never considered myself a complete musician; instead, I view myself as a work in progress. I'm constantly trying to become better. I can hardly say that there was ever a time when I was really able to play what I wanted to play. I have not reached that point really." "To play what I wanted to play"—but what is that? What is the goal of this endless searching? Even this was hard to make out, for himself as well as for the public. If the goal were clearly envisaged, then the perpetual changes would not have been looked upon as real inconsistency. But perhaps the goal simply cannot be defined—not, at least, in terms of musical, stylistic, or technical categories. "I'm not thinking about anything except reaching a point in my music where I can be happy with what I'm doing." (Giddins 1981, 120)

As long as that point remained out of reach, however, the self-criticism that could appear senseless, even masochistic to outsiders, grew steadily more severe. According to Ira Gitler's liner notes to *Tenor Madness*, one of his masterpieces, Rollins could only shake his head after each take and mutter, "Nothing's happening..." Over the years such pessimism developed into a true studio neurosis: self-criticism became self-obstruction. "If the essence of jazz is improvisation, then the whole concept of recording–freezing a particular moment and calling it definitive–violates that essence. And Sonny, who is the most intuitive musician I've ever met as well as the most intellectual, is the musician most acutely aware of that contradiction." Thus Orrin Keepnews, Rollins' producer in the '50s (and again in the '70s). (Davis 1986, 127) The conflict between focus and spontaneity–a common cause of discontent. But Rollins points out an additional one: the shadow of his own greatness, which makes him judge each improvisation by his earlier great performances. "Somewhere along the way I began to become very concerned about wanting to leave a really good recorded legacy, and I was very concerned about all of the notes coming out right. That has persisted up to the present time. I'm not very comfortable in the recording studio." (Jarrett 1990, 6) Such unease in the studio naturally affects the product–the recording: "There are a lot of records I don't even listen to, because I can't stand to listen to myself"–a judgment on his own body of work that is as puzzling as it is characteristic.

That artists are often their own harshest critics is well known and should not by itself be taken as indicating a lack of self-confidence. Criticism by others is another story. Rollins has proved susceptible to this too–so much so, that one is again put in mind of the image of the vulnerable giant. In 1961 he told Joe Goldberg: "You understand I won't read whatever you write... I read all the magazines when they were writing about me. I began to worry about things I shouldn't have. People said that I did a certain thing and I began to believe them, and by the time I figured out how I did it, I was unable to achieve the effect any more." (Goldberg 1965a, 102) The centipede that can longer walk once it has begun to think about how its legs move... There are, to be sure, other, less abstract reasons for Rollins' sensitivity to published criticism. Thus his reply to Art Taylor, when asked whether a negative notice bothers him: "Yes, it does. I don't have the greatest opinion of myself; I recognize a lot of my faults. They might contain something that's accurate, a good point that I can dig. But as a rule, I don't like a bad write-up because it would affect my name, whether or not it's right… This is affecting my economic life. I have to kinda get a good review in order to be able to work." (Taylor 1983, 169)

One can remain immune to negative reviews by refusing to read them. Musical fashions, on the other hand, are harder to ignore. And here the impressionability of Sonny Rollins the musical giant is more obvious. "I don't want anything dated, I don't want to sound like a museum piece. That's not my thing. I mean, I'm not a bebop player. I can play bebop, I came up in the bebop period, that's when I was growing up, and bebop is the greatest music that there is, as far as that's concerned, but I don't want to be thought of as a bebop player–I think who I am is more than that." He certainly is "more than that." Rollins, who brought Caribbean elements into jazz, who has transformed the most unpromising show and music-hall tunes into jazz treasures–the fact that he never accepted preconceived ideas about what one should or should not do as a jazz musician is well established. His music in fact is, in his own words, "beyond the idiom"–it transcends the boundaries of a narrow view of jazz (Giddins 1981, 120). Not all his stylistic waywardness, though, can be explained in terms of his own background, his musical biography, as these examples can. Sometimes he seems to have been motivated by circumstances, by the musical Zeitgeist. "When I started back in the seventies, I experienced a situation where a lot of my friends were not playing anymore, or dead. So for me to get a band I had to hire young people, and these young people, well, they liked jazz, they respected me and respected other people like Miles and Coltrane, they knew about Monk and all of this stuff, but they still liked the electric music of the day. I tried to use them. I mean, I had no choice, I had to use these young musicians. So I used them and tried to get what I could from playing with them." (Wilson 1988, 10) Rollins seemed to have formulated no very definite ideas of how his own music should sound in future: "Anything I play is going to come out Sonny in some kind of way." (Berg, 38) This underlying certainty may account for the apparent casualness with which Rollins, especially since the '70s, has gone about choosing his repertoire and personnel.

His participation on the Rolling Stones LP *Tattoo You* shows how open Sonny can be to outside influences when making artistic decisions. "I was not familiar with their work... My wife liked them. She thought that they were the best rock band around. She kind of convinced me: 'Well listen to them...' I looked at it, 'Well, let me see if I can...' I know I can play me, but I want to play something that fits into what this is about." (Jarrett 1990, 8) An unusual case, to be sure, but probably not an isolated instance in Rollins' oeuvre. He sometimes gives the impression that he is downright happy to have questions of style and repertoire taken out of his hands–whether by colleagues, or by his wife Lucille: "She's a real straight arrow. She keeps me in line. Left to my own devices, I can get pretty wild." (Porter 1974, 15) Thus he describes the influence Lucille has on him–a moderating influence, a shield against excess. And it is probably fair to see this moderating influence in his music as well as his private life. Since 1981 she has acted as co-producer of Rollins' recordings, and even on earlier albums she is sometimes given "special thanks from the producer" Orrin Keepnews "for influence and taste" (cover of *Don't Stop the Carnival*). She tends to the editing and mixing of the studio tapes along with the recording engineer (and without her husband's involvement). Obviously then, she exercises considerable control over Sonny's representation on record. But his involvement in the Rolling Stones production suggests that she also influences his repertoire. One can characterize the nature of this influence in broad terms as tending to emphasize the popular side of Rollins' style, to help make him accessible to a larger, pop-oriented public. That this is not mere speculation is supported by his explanation as to why he assigns the artistically crucial process of mixing a record to his wife: "I leave that to Lucille... She has the common touch that's necessary for mixing; she hears things the way a lot of people would hear them, in terms of sounds, levels, and so on." (Cioe, 77). To put it another way: Lucille Rollins is the public envoy who attunes the music of her husband to the attitudes and expectations of a wider audience. It would be pushing it to ascribe his turn to fusion music since the beginning of the '70s alone to her "influence and taste," but it is safe to assume she supported the move.

body and soul

The image of the wavering giant must, of course, take into account the "sabbaticals," as Rollins himself calls them—the periods in which he withdrew from the jazz scene completely. "I've got my life laid out in a much better way now," Rollins said in 1982 (Blumenthal 1982, 18). "I'm working, but I'm not constantly out there, and I can relax when I'm not working and prepare for the next time." It was just this balance that was lacking in earlier years. "Before it was either/or, now it's not quite like that." And it was just this "either/or" that once made his career so unpredictable: either there was feverish activity—especially in the years 1956–1959, when he played on over 30 LPs—or years of self-enforced silence.

The causes behind the three sabbaticals of 1954/55, 1959–1961, and 1969–1971 differ, no doubt, depending on his personal and musical circumstances. And yet there are common features—features that involve goals which Rollins over the course of decades constantly pursued, though with shifting strategies that sometimes puzzled his public. One constant: during the periods of retreat, physical, mental, and artistic renewal always went hand in hand. The physical, drug-dependency problems—the effects of heroin, alcohol, and amphetamines—were sometimes the immediate cause for pulling back from the grinding routine of the jazz musician. But afterwards emerged a man rejuvenated as much in mind as body.

"Nothing has changed very much as far as I can see"—that's how Rollins responded in 1961 to the question of what it was like to be back on the scene. "But *I've* changed ... I know that some people will be disappointed that I haven't come back on the scene with some brand new thing..., but I did come back with a brand new thing–me." (Coss 1962, 13) What distinguishes this 'new me'? At the very least, allegiance to a religion, a belief, a school, movement, or political party. Rollins' self-reclamation program in 1961 followed along such lines. As he revealed to *Down Beat* journalist Bill Coss, he had joined the Rosicrucians, a secret society whose origins lay in the Middle Ages. "It's a science, not a religion, and it's given me a lot of strengths, maybe developed them, that I didn't know I had before." (Coss 1962, 13) Later, towards the end of the decade, Zen and yoga were invoked as passwords to his spiritual renewal. But over the years, labels such as Rollins the Rosicrucian, Rollins the Zen Buddhist, have become blurred. To Art Taylor's question, put to him in 1971, whether he was religious, he answered noncommittally: "I've been religious at times; then I thought I might be on the wrong track when things went against the way I thought they should be... I haven't met anyone who really knows anything about religion. No one knows. I would like to believe, I would like to feel that there's something worthwhile and that there is a God. I have to say at this point in my life, I don't know." (Taylor 1983, 169f.) When Brian Priestley interviewed him in 1988 in his New York apartment and asked about the thick stack of very miscellaneous religious literature on his nightstand, Rollins said, "Yeah, I sort of am a religionist in the way that I study a lot, you know. When I went to India, I was into yoga, and then I was into Zen when I was in Japan... It's just interesting to me, the different religions and so on. I found a lot of things that I could relate to, as anyone else would, I'm sure, in all the religions. But I haven't found one that's for me. I mean, there's so much abuse of different religions. I mean, men are so imperfect that they abuse a lot of these things. So I don't want to be part of any established religious group, no. But I like to see the inspired works of people in all of the religions, and find the common thread, you know." (Priestley 1988, 34)

And this is anything but an abstract interest. Rollins the musician, and Rollins the amateur student of religion–this is a false distinction. "Spirituality is nothing I had to acquire. I have always believed anyway, deep down..." (Fiofori 1971, 14) Spirituality for him is not just a search for meaning, it's a practical search for ways to mentally manage the everyday life of a jazz musician. Asked by a Japanese journalist what attracted him to Zen, he answered: "The aspect of gaining control of living and the material part of being," adding, "Someday I hope to be a saint." (*Down Beat,* 12/19/63) If Rollins sets less lofty spiritual goals today, or expresses doubt about reaching transcendental certainties, eastern wisdom has still enabled him to find ways to regulate his life, in body and soul, to ground his existence as a creative artist in the rat race of the music profession. For this was probably the decisive lesson of his extended stays in India and Japan. "You can't escape yourself. The main thing is to get your head together so that you can function wherever you're at, at your optimum. So what I discovered was that I still had to deal with things as they existed in the States, or wherever I might be. I had hoped that I would get a lot of esoteric secrets about life, but it didn't quite work out that way. What I did find out is that you have to deal with things wherever you are." (Berg 1977, 38)

For Rollins, then, spirituality is not escapism, not mental retreat from a reality he finds intolerable. It is ultimately a strategy for mastering this reality. An essential, perhaps decisive, part of this quest involved his encounter with the *Bhagavadgita*, the Hindu didactic poem. "But what made me come back was... well, I realized that the only thing that I could really do, do as well as I could do it was music. It seems a simple thing to say, but it's not that simple in actuality. There was nothing else I really cared for enough to want to get into as a way of living. So I said, 'Well, this is it. Music is it.' Also, when I went to India, there was a book called the *Bhagavadgita*, which has to do with looking for your particular niche in life, what you want to do, what you should do, as a matter of fact. In effect, it says that there's certain things that you are meant to do, you have talent to do it, you have ability to do it, it's better to do that than to try do to something else which might appear to you to be a higher step—but it's better to sort of do what you know you should be doing. Now music is something I knew I had, people liked my music, I knew I had talent in it, I knew I had made a contribution in music. All of this dawned on me, and as I said, I wasn't really equipped to do other things."

"Action itself is the object, never the success of that action. Do not allow success to become the goal of action, but do not hope to avoid action either." Thus does Krishna advise the warrior Arjuna in the second *canto* of the *Bhagavadgita*. Action instead of inaction—but action devoid of ambition. To abstain from acting and withdraw into passivity—that would be a mistake. "Never does man enjoy freedom from action by not undertaking action, nor does he attain that freedom by mere renunciation of action. For no one ever remains inactive even for a moment; the nature inherent in us forces everyone to act. And so accomplish your allotted task; for action is better than inaction." (*Bhagavadgita,* third *canto*)

Rollins could evidently apply such words to his own case when he withdrew from musical activity in 1969 and tended only to his spiritual interests. "He who performs all obligatory action, without relying on the success thereof, that man is a sage and an ascetic–not the man who renounces action." (*Bhagavadgita,* sixth *canto*) "It is not right to renounce one's allotted task. Its abandonment, from delusion, is said to be ignorance. Whoever abandons action because it is painful or strains one's limbs–such a man will never gain the fruit of his abandonment. But when an allotted task is performed from a sense of duty and without desire or hope of success, such abandonment is blessed." (*canto* 18)

But which actions are "allotted," and wherein does "duty" lie? The poem has an answer to that too: "One's own duty, however unpleasant, is better than somebody else's duty which may be more easy to perform. Doing duty that accords with one's nature–then one is blameless." (*canto* 18) To remain true to one's essence, to devote oneself to the activity one is destined for–in Rollins' case, that could only mean one thing, a renewed commitment to music.

To music, yes–but not to the musical grind. Which is what these few citations from the *Bhagavadgita* entail: the injunction to tend to one's proper action goes hand in hand with the command to find a new attitude to one's vocation–'renouncing desire and success', i.e., never allowing success to be the motive for action. In Rollins' case that meant nothing less than the challenge of approaching jazz, a music that privileges the ego and the individual, in a spirit of self-sacrifice: a paradoxical challenge, to be sure. And perhaps it is just this search for selflessness in a music of extreme self-referentiality that makes Rollins' music since the '70s–since his Eastern travels–sometimes seem unfocused. Sonny Rollins has involved himself in the life of a musician again, but has done so, one might say, in a disinterested manner–without the ambition of drawing attention to himself by always striving for something new or revolutionary–in the consciousness alone, that in the musical world as it is presently constituted he is doing what he is fated to do by birth and education. What at first may seem casual or haphazard in his approach, on a higher plane reveals itself to be the purest consistency: Always remaining true to himself.

the loner

"I'm a private person who does not even like to be out socializing." (Blumenthal 1982, 18) Indeed: it seems that Rollins has arranged his life so as to minimize contact with other people, even other musicians. Since the early '70s he lives with his wife and his pets on a small farm in Germantown, approximately 100 miles north of New York City. In New York City he keeps a small apartment that serves as office and domicile during his sporadic visits into town. To strangers–journalists, for instance–he is friendly, patient, and ready to volunteer information, but usually so reserved that one leaves conscious of having seen only his public persona. Even with his sidemen he maintains his distance. Rollins and his sidemen–for that's what they are, for all his talk of musical *égalité*–often travel separately, and stay in different hotels. And he apparently does not seek out opportunities to meet other musicians. On tour he spends most of his time in his hotel, reading, doing yoga, or watching TV. "Sonny doesn't hang out"–that's how vocalist Betty Carter (born the same year as Sonny) succinctly puts it. News of what's happening on the jazz scene reaches him only by chance, at second hand, through his fellow players, who are without exception much younger than he. That may come as a surprise from a musician who was once open to the most various musical encounters, who opened himself to the *new thing*–especially one who in his stage presence and his playing evinces a unique readiness to communicate.

And yet his aloofness may only be a response to those personal problems that he had to struggle with when he returned to the scene–problems that used to culminate in dependence on drugs of various kinds. If his solitary habits as a person tend to reinforce Sonny's more solitary traits as a musician–even to the point of autism, to judge from his indifference to current musical trends–that is probably the price to be paid for a measure of psychic self-protection.

This detachment, even apart from the "sabbaticals," has also kept Rollins from attaining the status of musical leader that some had envisaged for him. "Needed Now: Sonny Rollins." That's how Gordon Kopulos in 1971 lead off an article in *Down*

Beat, in which he projected Sonny in the role of mediator on a jazz scene torn between jazz-rock commercialism and avant-garde cultism. But Rollins has always ducked this role, to the consternation of some of his fans. "It's a shame the man is that way," Arrigo Polillo says. "If Sonny Rollins were less unpredictable, less tormented by existential problems, less unsure of himself and better adjusted, he would certainly be the great figure of jazz in the 1970s. But he doesn't want to be... To be a leader, you at least have to have the desire to show other people the way, to win others over, and that's never been something Rollins wanted to do." (Polillo 1981, 566) Sonny even had problems as head of his own ensembles since 1957 when he first began leading them. Not just the practical problems of dealing with agents and clubowners, and managing finances, but, far more serious (because you can't delegate it), the difficulty of putting and holding together a group of stylistically compatible musicians who have something to say in their solos and yet get along well as a group. Unlike his friend and rival Coltrane, another one of the great 'seekers' of modern jazz, Sonny Rollins the lone wolf has not succeeded in that. It may be that he was simply too uncertain about his own music to put up with strong musical personalities alongside him for very long.

call to freedom or *l'art pour l'art*? the Freedom Suite

"America has deep roots in the culture of the blacks: in their idioms, their humor, their music. How ironic, then, that the black man, who has a greater claim on America's culture than anyone else, is persecuted and oppressed; that the black man, who is an example to humanity through his mere existence, is rewarded for it with inhumanity." The *Freedom Suite* of 1958, on whose jacket these statements by Rollins are found, seems to have been the first unequivocal musical-political statement in jazz. It was, as Rollins later explained, motivated by his own experience of the schizophrenia felt by the successful black artist in the United States. "I wrote it at a time when I was beginning to get a lot of good publicity, and everyone was hailing me and saying how great I was. Yet when I went to look for a good apartment, I ran into this same old stuff. Here I had all these reviews, newspaper articles and pictures. I can look back on it and see that it was a natural thing we all go through. At the time it struck me, what did it all mean if you were still a nigger, so to speak? This is the reason I wrote the suite." (Taylor 1983, 171 ff.)

The *Freedom Suite* coincided with the beginning of a period of self-assertion among black musicians. It would assume more definite form in Charles Mingus' *Fables of Faubus*, Archie Shepp's *Poem to Malcolm* and the "Great Black Music" proclamations of the Art Ensemble of Chicago. Was Rollins, then, the prototype of the political musician? He has been eloquent on the subject of "music and politics"—especially in recent years—but as a programmatic statement the *Freedom Suite* is pretty much an isolated instance in his *oeuvre*. His statements to *Down Beat* journalist Bill Coss in 1961 are still quasi-political, but conciliatory: Jazz, he says, should play an important part in the efforts toward peace in the world, because it represents freedom and cooperation (Coss 1962, 14). And how does it contribute to that? "My place is to bring happiness and joy to the public with what I–we–play. This is what we hope to accomplish. It's obvious how I feel about the racial problem. I'll do my job–on the stand, with my instrument." (*Down Beat*, 12/19/63) Music brings joy and happiness into the world: if this is a political view of music, it can be regarded so only in a traditional, even conservative sense: music as a distraction from the pressures of reality. This is not unfair to Rollins: "Music should be judged on what it is. It should be very high and above everything else. It is a beautiful way of bringing people together, a little bit of an oasis in this messed-up world. If I look at it like that, then I have to reject the idea of trying to put politics into music." (Taylor 1983, 172) More distinctly: "Everything I try to do when I get on the stand is anti-politics... Music should make people forget about politics–people fighting other people for positions. Music should be the antithesis of all these other things." (Jarrett 1990, 6f.)

This sounds like a defense of art for art's sake, and a retreat from the strong political positions that characterized the '60s. But one should not forget that it represents only the media face of Sonny Rollins–and that, like every artist, he has developed in the course of the decades strategies to reveal only those facets of his thought and personality that he wants the public to see. Anyone who has ever spoken with, or even read interviews by, this polite but reserved man, realizes this at once. There is one interview, however, that gives occasional glimpses of the man behind the mask. It comes from the collection that drummer Art Taylor, a childhood friend of Sonny's, published under the title "Notes and Tones. Musician-to-Musician Interviews." What he says here regarding his view of politics and the race question in particular goes so far beyond his usual noncommittal statements as to leave little doubt that in interviews the questioner is often more important than the questions. Rollins is naturally much more confiding with his friend from Sugar Hill than with a white journalist (whose writings he had probably not read a word of before they met).

"I'll say this—about ten years ago I used to be very much in favor of trying to bridge the gap between white and black. I used to read a lot of philosophy and look for ways of bringing everybody together. I would go out of my way to try and make friends. But now I know that this is redundant on my part as a black man, because it's not up to me to do it; it's up to the white man to be friendly with me. If I do it, the white cat can say it's because I want to better my position in the world. It can be looked upon as a selfish thing. I can't go around to the guy preaching love and let's get together, because it can be looked upon as being suspect coming from a black cat. Do you understand what I mean? It's a white person's prerogative to do all of these things; I can't do it. I had to give up that idea because it really doesn't work. It's up to the ruling class, so to speak, to do all of these things. It's probably to the advantage of a white person to keep himself on top and the black below, so I honestly can't see why a white person would want to change things." (Taylor 1983, 171)

style

the secret of sonny's sound

"Even if you have some brilliant jazz ideas, it's going to be difficult to get them across unless you have (a) a distinctive sound or (b) a loud sound. These are musts." (Jarrett 1990, 7) As this quote makes clear, Sonny Rollins is himself fully aware of the importance of a distinctive saxophone sound–and there is no doubt that his sound meets both criteria: strength and individuality.

The pianist Paul Bley remembers: "One night at the Open Door [in New York], Rollins was working with Art Blakey and a bassist as a trio. Blakey's forte, as you know, was playing thirty choruses, each louder than the one before. Rollins knew this and started climbing slowly with Blakey until they got to the top of Art's volume. Then Sonny climbed about twenty more choruses volume-wise." (Lyons 1983, 161) It may be that such anecdotes exaggerate to make a point; but that Rollins is among the tenorists with a powerful sound is well established. (In the Jarret interview he remarks that in his early years he had to play against a large band without benefit of a microphone.) From the beginning the volume and fullness of his sound distinguished him from the Lester Young school (to which he might otherwise be assigned on the basis of his phrasing). But of course it is not just strength that makes Sonny's sound distinctive; he has put it best himself: "I'm a speech-like player. My phrasing and everything, it's more speech-like than it is legato, though I like to do things legato also. But what I play is very unorthodox, unusual... It's very percussive some of the time. Coleman Hawkins was like that, especially his early stuff. Way back he almost sounded like a guy talking. Of course Coleman was my idol, you know." (Rollins to David Weiss, quoted in the liner notes of *The Quartets*)

Here a crucial point about Rollins' distinctive sound—about the individuality of instrumental sound generally—is touched upon: sound is not static, but dynamic, a matter of formation. Just as one recognizes a speaker by their articulation, intonation, and personal inflections more readily than by the color of their voice, so the dynamic elements of articulation, phrasing, and tone production are critical to a horn player's sound. And where such micro-dynamics are concerned, Sonny Rollins has more resources than most saxophonists. In the view of David Baker (Baker 1980, 16), "He has perhaps the most widely varied articulation of any jazz player." One might suppose that a musician like Archie Shepp or Lester Bowie has equal claim to the title; a basic difference is that Rollins can give special weight to every note in a series through a rich array of techniques–from percussive, staccato articulation (a trademark of his playing, as he notes above), through suave half-swallows of the notes (so-called ghosted notes), through glissando effects leading to central pitches or away, to all shades of vibrato up to the bleating extreme. If there are common elements that justify his traditional assignment to the Coleman Hawkins/Ben Webster/Dexter Gordon school–the sheer fullness of sound, especially in the tenor's difficult lower end, the tendency toward robustness, particularly in fast tempi–it is still the wealth of micro-resources, the range of his speech-like inflections, that justify Rollins' position as one the great sound creators of modern jazz.

How variable Sonny's sound can be is evident not only on the small scale, in the finer points of inflection, but even in the broad outlines of his musical career. No simple, linear development can be traced. From one record to the next he sounds different, often even on successive tracks of the same LP. But two very broad trends can be identified: first, after the sixties Rollins' sound is essentially more varied than before the Bridge *intermezzo*; and secondly, his sound is usually broader, more nasal, less clearly sculpted than during the early years (even if the occasional performance from the later years evokes déja-vu (or déja-entendu) of Rollins in the late fifties). Both tendencies are plausibly related to some stylistic and biographical developments.

The increased flexibility in the area of color and articulation undoubtedly relates to his intense involvement since the end of the fifties with new playing techniques–activity that, as he reports, called into question such self-evident things as the saxophone as a monophonic instrument. "Like, one time some years back I was playing in a way where I wasn't playing any single lines. I was just playing double or triple notes and I was playing this way for a short period of time, and I was playing one time at the factory and one of the guys there said, 'When I was coming up that type of playing was considered wrong.' I'm just relating this to show that there is just so much that you can do with any horn. It's just that what might be considered wrong one day might be considered right the next." (Fiofori 1971, 15) (Echoes of this style of 'multiphonics' can be heard on "Jungoso," from the 1962 album *What's New*). In the sixties he experimented with double or triple notes, notes above the normal range ('high harmonics'), and subtle tone colorations. His detailed exploration of his instrument's tonal possibilities resulted in his sound spectrum becoming ever more diverse. As to the second tendency–toward a less clearly contoured, more nasal, sometimes blurry sound–this can be traced not only to technical experimentation, but to physical factors beyond his control–even in part to his struggle with drugs. "I use a medium reed today," Rollins told Bob Porter in 1974. (Porter 1974, 15) "Some years ago I used a very hard reed, but I've gotten away from that." The switch from hard reeds, which produce an especially rich and voluminous sound, but make great demands on one's face muscles, to softer, more tractable ones, will have been necessitated not least by some costly tooth treatments that Rollins underwent in the early sixties which forced him to stop playing for several months. As with John Coltrane, his addiction to heroin, long overcome, still affected him later on in the form of advanced tooth decay; and, like Coltrane, Rollins had to redevelop his embouchure after extensive dental work. The fact that since then he uses different mouthpieces is another factor contributing to the shifting Rollins sound. In the late fifties he usually used the metal mouthpieces manufactured by the firm of Otto Link, but since the seventies mainly a Berg-Larsen stainless steel one—while continually experimenting with other brands. "I interchange them depending on the condition of my chops. I think it is a good idea to change mouthpieces. You get into different sounds." (Porter 1974, 15)

And there's no limit to the experimentation. "The saxophone's such a unique instrument. It has this conical shape, which is very mystical, and it produces overtones which are very difficult to figure out in a scientific way. With a cylindrical instrument it's easy to see why the overtones do certain things. With a conical one, the overtones do things like—the music comes back into your throat and out again. It's a very mystical thing. I think there's a lot more that can be done." (Cook 1985, 31)

thematic, motivic?

Whoever regards musicological analysis as just idle theorizing in the ivory tower will know better after reading Gunther Schuller's analysis of Rollins in the November 1958 issue of *Jazz Review.* Entitled "Sonny Rollins and the Challenge of Thematic Improvisation," the article by the writer, conductor, composer, and third-stream pioneer not only helped determine the course of Rollins criticism for years to come, it even impressed Sonny: "I hadn't really understood how I played before I read Gunther Schuller," Rollins said later (whether seriously or with a wink, is open to question), adding, "This business about the thematic approach–I think it's correct, but I had never thought about it; I just played it." Still, Schuller's essay had its downside, in that reflection on the essence of his own playing tended to make Rollins self-conscious, and impede the free flow of his invention (as attested by statements quoted in the previous chapter).

Schuller's premise, now a commonplace, that Rollins was the pioneer of 'thematic' improvisation, must be looked at closely, because like many received ideas it involves some distortion along with a kernel of truth. "Today we have reached another juncture in the constantly unfolding evolution of improvisation, and the central figure of this present renewal is Sonny Rollins," Schuller asserts at the start of his essay (Schuller 1986, 86) What, according to Schuller, distinguishes the saxophonist's manner? "Something Sonny Rollins has contributed decisively to the spectrum of jazz improvisation, is the idea of developing and varying the main theme, not just a secondary motif that the player haphazardly uses in the course of his improvisation and which in itself has no relation to the theme of the composition." (Schuller 1986, 96). Hence the phrase 'thematic improvisation' to designate Rollins' new (according to Schuller) and unique approach to improvisation over a given theme. Schuller grounds his hypothesis in an analysis of Rollins' solo in "Blue Seven" from June 1956 (on *Saxophone Colossus*). Especially in choruses 11 to 13–in Schuller's words, the 'coronation' of the extended solo–virtually all the saxophonist's phrases are based on the theme. "Such structural cohesiveness...one has come to expect from the composer who spends days or weeks writing a given passage. It is another matter to achieve this in an on-the-spur-of-the-moment extemporization." (p. 91)

Schuller's analysis is much quoted, or paraphrased, but rarely has its accuracy been reviewed; it seems jazz journalists implicitly trust this renowned representative of the classical muse, and are grateful for his validation of jazz as a serious art form. But a closer look at Schuller's arguments gives rise to doubts—doubts, first, as to what his terminology involves. We can speak of 'thematic' improvisation in "Blue Seven"—and other pieces—only to a limited extent. It is true that Rollins at times is heard working certain motifs with remarkable persistence, but these motifs are certainly not all based on the simple riff of the blues theme. It would be better, then, to speak of "motivic" improvisation. Doubtful too, is Schuller's choice of material on which to build his case. There are indeed passages in "Blue Seven" in which Rollins improvises with motifs—but the parts analyzed by Schuller are only a fragment of the complete solo. And alongside "Blue Seven" you could compare countless other pieces in which he eschews motif- or theme-oriented playing to shape instead a mosaic of generally known and personal patterns, in the best bebop tradition. Finally, Schuller's historical claim is open to doubt: motivic or thematically structured improvisations were certainly not invented by Sonny Rollins, but can be traced in the tradition from Louis Armstrong through Thelonious Monk—the latter would certainly have been a big influence on Rollins in this regard. (It is true, however, that motif-oriented improvisation played only a minor role in the bop and hard-bop mainstream prior to Rollins.)

It would be hasty to declare Schuller's analysis invalid on the basis of these objections, and, with Barry Kernfeld, to conclude: "Rollins, like most bop musicians of the period, paid little attention to composed melodies, preferring instead to improvise athematic, 'formulaic' responses to underlying chord progressions." (Kernfeld 1988, 391) Because if Schuller's interpretation is flawed, nevertheless thematic improvisation *is* a characteristic approach in Rollins' playing—one of several, to be sure, but one he has remained faithful to until today, and one that is actually more typical of his recordings in the sixties, seventies, and eighties than the performance that Schuller analyzed.

This can be established from some chronological sampling. The starting point of Rollins' stylistic evolution was undoubtedly (in this respect Kernfeld was right) the pattern approach to soloing that Charlie Parker first perfected. The soloist draws upon (mainly standard) melodic solutions to given harmonic situations. Rollins' solo on the blues "Hi-Lo," recorded in 1949 with J.J. Johnson (music example 1) is an example of this typical bebop solo (including some very typical Parker phrases, marked by brackets in the transcription, phrases that he shared with many of his contemporaries and only discarded toward the end of the 50s.) (Note: music example 1 is, like all the others, notated at sounding pitch.) There is no sign of thematic or motivic improvisation in Schuller's sense. A slightly later example—"Newk's Fadeaway" from 1951—shows the application of this procedure to the 32-bar "rhythm changes"

music example 1: solo in "Hi-Lo" (1949)

model, along with some personal variations on the art of the bebop pattern mosaic: Rollins' penchant for simple diatonic passages, for instance, is here, along with individual touches like the characteristic cadenza phrase with augmented dominant chord (music example 2). This blueprint applies to many of Rollins' improvisations in the following years; alongside it, however, especially after 1955, solos increasingly appear in which Rollins works with defined motifs over one or more choruses–whether the material derives from the theme or is

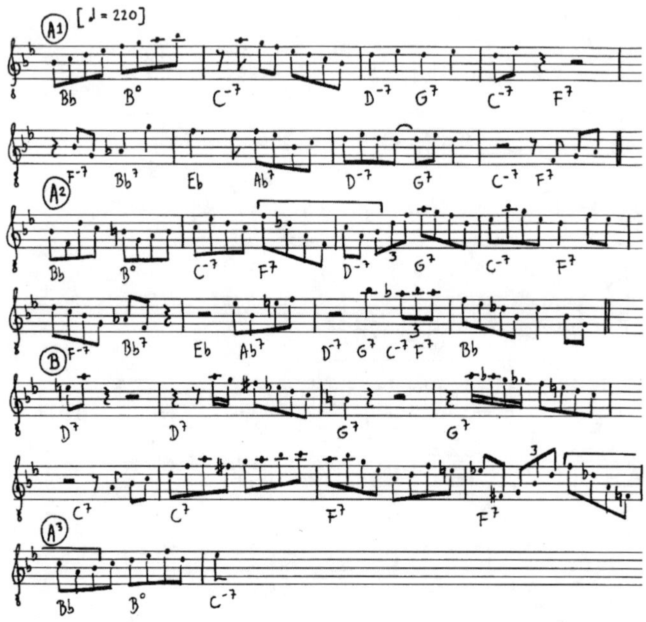

music example 2: "Newk's Fadeaway," 2nd chorus (1951)

itself improvised. The first choruses over "St. Thomas" from June 1956 actually provide an even more compelling example of thematic improvisation than Schuller's paradigm case, "Blue Seven" (from the same album). The rising fourth G–C, with which the calypso theme begins, is inverted by Rollins into a descending fifth, which–compressed to a tritone, to a fourth, and finally to a major second–becomes the germ of his set of improvised variations (music example 3). It's clear from such examples that Rollins had taken the motto of his mentor Thelonious Monk to heart: "If you know the melody, you can make a better solo"–i.e. one should play with the melody, not

music example 3: “St. Thomas” (1956), 1st and beginning of 2nd chorus

just the chords. This is even more obvious on the version of “Brilliant Corners” he recorded a few months later, where Rollins makes Monk’s basic theme the foundation for his bold arabesques (music example 4; as with the other transcriptions, Sonny’s highly nuanced microrhythm and timing can only be roughly indicated.)

The motivic or thematic approach was only one of Rollins’ techniques in the fifties, and hardly the dominant one, but in the years following the famous sabbatical of 1959–61 it gains noticeably in prominence. If you compare the recordings of the sixties with those of the previous decade, you almost get the impression that in those two years of practice and experimentation he explicitly set himself the task of becoming fully

music example 4: “Brilliant Corners” (1956): theme above, Rollins’ improvisation below

conscious of his own patterns, his own melodic and rhythmic tendencies–and of banishing them from his playing. "Now I can play what I want to play," Rollins said in 1962 to *Down Beat* journalist Bill Coss (Coss 1962, 14), and this new-found confidence may relate to his liberation from a self-sustaining repertoire of patterns and riffs. In place of this style manual–whatever 'lies to hand'–a kind of improvisational fluency succeeds that Rollins called 'stream of consciousness' (Berg 1977, 39). And this stream of consciousness often avails itself of the theme for its starting point, sometimes paraphrasing it or abandoning it for side excursions, but returning to it again and again. Rollins' solo on the theme of "Alfie" is a classic example of this new method, which derives its characteristic tension from the alternation of thematically bound passages with others that drastically negate the motivic and harmonic foundations. (Musical example 5 excerpts two such contrasting sections). Today Rollins gives his sidemen the following directions on how to play: "No, we're not going to do that, we're not going to play melody and stop and then solo and chords, we're going to continually develop the melody over and over and over again. So this is the way I think, this is the modus operandi of my improvising. I mean, I want to develop, I don't want to go into changes and the stop and go back to the melody–I mean, it's all one piece, an organic process." (Wilson 1988, 9)

Of course, this is no recipe and Rollins himself hardly regards it as such. In the recordings from the seventies, especially, Rollins' solos often hew so closely to the theme that a sense of restricted improvisational flight overshadows the

music example 5: a chorus from "Keep Hold of Yourself" (1972)

thematic stringency. (One example: the title piece from *The Cutting Edge* (1974). It should also be noted that during these years the modal scales which became popular after Coltrane also found a place in Rollins' style–pentatonic scales especially, as in the blues "Keep Hold of Yourself" (from *Next Album,* 1972–music example 5). (It is notable that, as in his use of the soprano sax, such obvious Coltrane influences only emerged years after the death of his close colleague.) Judged by his own high standards, Rollins' relatively uninspired improvisations on modal pieces suggest that the great melodist needs the pull of a chord progression, the directionality of a cadenza, to inspire his powers of motivic formulation.

What role do patterns, or set phrases–be they his own or another's–have in Rollins' playing today? He has not totally banished them from his playing, as he probably once resolved to do. He has only refused to limit himself to them. He can resort to them on occasion, but will transcend them with equal ease; and this virtuosity above and beyond a facility with formulas is what sets Rollins apart from such contemporaries as Johnny Griffin and Sonny Stitt.

music example 6: the first saxophone chorus of "Vierd Blues" (1956)

the organizer of space

"His most dramatic device was his rushing, lagging, or floating over the beat; he seemed to disengage from, expand or contract the pulse at will. The sense of rhythmic liberation is enormous." (Litweiler 1984, 20) While the significance of thematic improvisation for Rollins' personal style may be debated, his contribution to the rhythmic emancipation of the jazz soloist is universally acknowledged. Jean Delmas has given him the fitting title "le grand organisateur des lacunes"—"the great organizer of space"—and contrasted him with John Coltrane, "the man of amplitude" (a contrast surely more valid than the one commonly found in the literature between Coltrane the innovator and Rollins his conservative counterpart).

This mastery in the handling of musical time, of sound and silence, characterizes Rollins' improvisations since the first 'comeback' of 1955, following the fluent, but rhythmically conservative and rather monotonous solos of the early years.

music example 7: "Sonnymoon for Two," live version (1957)

Here again we may detect the influence of Thelonious Monk, that wizard of time, who Rollins frequently played with during this period. A case study: the first two choruses of "Vierd Blues," recorded in March of 1956 (music example 6). The first thing we notice is the calmness with which he starts his solo; a single note suffices for the first four bars. Only in the eighth and ninth bar do we get a sense of linear development—and then merely a glimpse. Nowhere do we get the string of eighth notes alternating with triplets that typified bebop. Silence here is just as important as sound—as a dramatic element, even more important. The jagged, unpredictable rhythmic structure led one puzzled Rollins critic to speak of "the agony of fragmentary idea lines" (Hadlock 1958, 49). Sparingly at first—and that much more effectively—Rollins introduces into the solo his sixteenth-note double-time virtuosity, developing it further in later choruses. All in all, the organization of sound and silence, of calmness and excitement, of rhythmic contrasts, mark Rollins' solo on "Vierd Blues" as a masterpiece—and alongside this rhythmic creativity the soloist still manages to maintain motivic continuity: the descending tritone, which opens the second chorus, runs through subsequent bars like a red thread.

In other solos, rhythm acquires a life of its own, independent of the melody. In the first three choruses of his solo in "Sonnymoon for Two," for instance, from the Village Vanguard recordings of November 1957, the descending fifth F–B (derived from the theme) is made the object of an exercise in rhythmic displacement, until the tension built up by ignoring the melody is released in liberating virtuoso runs (music example 7).

But Rollins' rhythmic command is not only evident in his solos. In his statement of the themes he often shows his skill in creating rhythmic tension, even hypertension. In the version of "How High The Moon" from Sweden, March of '59, he prolongs the first note of the theme to the point where you

music example 8: "How High the Moon": original theme above, Rollins below (1959)

think the interplay of the trio would fall to pieces; but the form of the piece is then rescued by an equally bold compression of the melody (music example 8).

Sometimes we find an analogy to this rhythmic displacement in the area of pitch. For example, on "There Will Never Be Another You" (recorded the same day), a fragment of the melody is displaced a half-note upwards for a time, an early instance of the "in-and-out" technique so popular with contemporary saxophonists.

eclectic eccentric–rollins' repertoire

Rollins' individuality is evident even before he starts presenting the themes–it is evident in the choice of themes themselves. The scope of his repertoire is amazing. Unlike other musicians from the bebop era–unlike his friend and mentor

Miles Davis, for example—Rollins has never limited himself to standards or his own compositions, or to variations on the usual blues and "I Got Rhythm" schemes. "So many musicians play the same few pieces again and again. There is so much music in the world that it is stupid to be content with only a small part of it." (Goldberg 1965a, 105) Tunes like "Toot, Toot, Tootsie," "I'm An Old Cowhand," "There's No Business Like Show Business," were very unorthodox vehicles for improvisational creativity in the '50s—and the "Tennessee Waltz," which he interprets on the 1989 CD *Falling in Love with Jazz*, is hardly more central to the jazz repertoire. He has recorded only a handful of compositions more than once—mainly calypso classics like "St. Thomas" and "Don't Stop the Carnival."

Impatience with his taste for popular music—much of it no longer popular—is tempered by the assumption made by jazz journalists then and now that a certain irony is intended; and the droll manner in which he treats some of these themes might indeed suggest that Rollins was merely parodying the material, making a kind of sly dig at popular music clichés. "Monk made me conscious how important it is to have a sense of humor in whatever you play"—so he writes in the liner notes of *Sonny Rollins and the Contemporary Leaders* from 1958. And if one thinks of the pianist's dry, unsentimental deconstruction of schmaltz like "Just a Gigolo," you might think that Rollins' revitalization of these faded hits also involves a kind of sardonic humor. Humor, he says, is actually a mainspring of his music: "I have a sense of humor. That gives me a kick in life. I'm a big fan of these [comedians] Bob and Ray. That influences my playing. I think I used to play a lot of practical jokes when I was in school. They used to call me

The Jester." (Jarret 1990, 6)

However, it would be simplistic to refer Rollins' eccentric taste in repertoire merely to his comic instinct. He says that personal history–nostalgia–is a factor in his choice of tunes: "I'm sure there's irony in my playing at times, but specifically to your question of why I play these songs... I knew a lot of these songs from my childhood. I liked music, I used to hear a lot of these songs on the radio... And I used to go to the movies a lot when we were kids; we used to go to the movies all the time, so I'd hear this movie music...and operettas, I used to see a lot of operetta–so melodies have always had an effect on me." Concerning his remarkable interpretation of a theme from Tchaikovsky's *Pathétique* in particular: "If I choose something to play on, it's something that I really like. I like the *Pathétique*. I mean, it's a nice piece of music, which can be done in a sort of jazz format, if you want to use that term, as well as the way it was written. So it in no way suggests any disrespect or trying to make fun of it–as a piece of music, it's something which I feel I can get something out of." How then to interpret his very personal, anything but "faithful," often downright irreverent treatment of the material? "It begins with an appreciation and a love of the material for what it is, and then I'm putting my interpretation to it." (Kalbacher 1988, 19)

"Jazz is not limited, as people think it is. That's why I played some of the songs that people thought were strange." (Goldberg 1965a, 105) Rollins' repertoire, true to his credo, has at various times encompassed film scores, calypso, semi-classical, and pop hits. But so-called standards, the basic inventory of modern jazz, have never wholly vanished from his concerts and CDs. (It is notable that it was precisely in his most avant-garde years—1962 to 1966—that Rollins played more standards than ever in his career, and fewer of his own numbers.) "The average Joe knows just as much as I do—he knows *more* than I do. *I'm* the average Joe, and I think people recognize that. That's why I play standards. Everybody knows 'Stardust.' These guys who only play their own tunes, they can cover up a lot of things, but if you play the melody of 'Stardust,' everybody can tell whether you're doing it right or not... How can you call yourself a professional musician if you don't know all those songs?" (Goldberg 1965b, 20) Standards, then, as the common ground among fans and musicians—that case could probably still be made in 1965, but today it is less persuasive. How many people at a Rollins' concert today would know the melody of "Stardust"? This shift in listener consciousness is an important motive for the constant turnover in his repertoire. If he still revisits the classic themes and forms of jazz, two reasons may be adduced. Like Monk, he is a musician whose creativity flourishes most in the framework of traditional structures—by playing *with*, not *in*, the tradition, as Ekkehard Jost has put it. (Jost 1975, 161) Rollins is very aware of history, and is always looking for a synthesis of old and new in his music. "I like to think that jazz can be played in a way that you can hear the old as well as the new. At least that's how I try to play and what I do personally... I listen to Louis Armstrong and hear something that I want to be able to hear in anything that's called 'jazz.'" (Blumenthal 1982, 18)

the new rollins—pluralism or populism?

Sonny Rollins confronted the challenges posed by the popularity of rock, and the increasing marginalization of jazz, later than Miles Davis, but earlier than Ornette Coleman. Like Davis' *Bitches Brew* (1969) and Coleman's *Dancing In Your Head* (1976), Rollins' *Next Album* inevitably split his fan base into nostalgic traditionalists, on the one hand, and supporters of the new, 'up-to-date' direction on the other—with the obligatory debate over progress and populism, innovation or accommodation. Unlike Davis or Coleman, however, Rollins did not change radically. Alongside new titles in the fusion mode he always kept bop-oriented pieces and ballads in the program.

For Rollins' apologists it was easy to defend the incorporation of rock rhythms and electric instruments as just the latest instance of that musical eclecticism he had always cultivated. Why not fusion today, when there had been calypso, film music, parlor classics, and Broadway hits in the past? Rollins' new-found enthusiasm for the soul-sax ecstasies of Junior Walker ("I love Jr. Walker's playing!" (Cioe 1983, 78) could even be interpreted as a revival of his childhood devotion to Louis Jordan.

Rollins justified the shift in style he undertook in the seventies in various ways, and not always consistently. Commercial considerations seem uppermost when he says, "But you have to think about whether or not it will reach audiences and whether it will sell." (Berg 1977, 38)—and he admits to 'mild' pressure on the part of his record company in this regard (although he resisted Milestone's suggestion to make an album of old rock hits after participating on the Stones' *Tattoo You.* (Cook 1985, 30)) And he explains the hiring of young, fusion-oriented musicians as simple necessity: "When I came back in the seventies, I experienced a situation where a lot of my old friends were not playing anymore, or dead. So for me to get a band I had to hire young people, and these young people, well, they liked jazz, they respected me and respected other people like Miles and Coltrane..., but they still liked a lot of this electric music of the day." On the other hand, it is likely that the new sounds–and specifically, the new rhythms–held a genuine fascination for Rollins: "I've always been a very rhythmic player, and I want the rhythms beneath me to be rhythms you can feel throughout your entire system, not just something you can tap your foot to. I know that some people think I should be using a fifties kind of rhythm section, with upright bass walking a straight four beats to the measure, the piano blocking out chords, and the drummer going 'ta-da, ta-da' or whatever, very discreetly in his cymbals. But that's tired, and it just doesn't appeal to me anymore. I want energy and constant propulsion, and I find only young players can give that to me." (Davis 1986, 127f.) And: "[The young musicians] are playing a new way, especially bass players; and this new rhythm grabs me." (Childs 1980, 32) So Rollins' stylistic change is 'over-determined' by several factors: commercial considerations, reluctance to turn into a living bebop museum, fascination with new forms of musical expression, a consciousness that as a musician it is his job to bring pleasure to the public–and eclecticism as a deliberate programme. "Each style gives me something to play off and relate to... If it were just up to me and not a matter of having to accommodate a band

and its abilities, I'd like to be more eclectic." (Cioe 1983, 90)

But the stylistic makeover met with a mixed response in the seventies. In the words of Gary Giddins, a critic generally sympathetic to Rollins: "As the seventies took shape, there appeared to be not one Sonny Rollins but two. The dynamic pathfinder of the concerts and nightclubs justified all the talk of pushing beyond the past, the edge, the self, the idiom, and left audiences palsied with pleasure and awe. A stony doppelganger deposited strangely timorous echoes of the real thing in a series of unfailingly disappointing (though often interesting) records." (Giddins 1981, 123) Giddins also questions the commercial logic of his stylistically and qualitatively heterogeneous record production: "The crazy thing is that every type of jazz demographics suggests that Rollins would sell more records to a coalition of long-time admirers and devoted young followers than to the dilettantes to which his compromised albums presumably pander." (Giddins 1981, 129) Not just the commercial, but also the musical logic of this new direction is doubtful. In the words of Francis Davis: "He talks as though there are no options beyond bop and fusion, which is simply not the case." Why doesn't he see that there are alternatives between hidebound traditionalism, and capitulation to fashion? Davis: "Talking to him, one gets the impression that he no longer monitors developments in jazz the way he did when he was younger–or the way Coleman Hawkins did throughout his career." (Davis 1986, 128)

The impression I got from my long conversation with him tends to confirm that Rollins, the lone wolf, who mainly hides out on his farm north of New York and has limited social contact, takes only mild interest in the current jazz scene, and is too involved in his own music to take much notice of others'. The question, for instance, as to who among the younger saxophonists he thinks he has influenced, drew an obvious blank. If Rollins' recordings since *Sunny Days, Starry Nights* (1984) have helped to overcome doubt about his new direction and bring his vision of an eclectic but valid music "beyond the idiom" (Giddins 1981, 120) closer to realization, it may be because he has learned one thing in the course of his musical odyssey: "I find that when I'm really playing myself, that's when I reach the audience. Trying to do anything else, I realized a long time ago, is counterproductive." (Jarrett 1990, 5)

the loneliness of the maestro

The authority of Rollins' playing predestined him to be a leader. According to the hierarchical laws of the jazz business, in which co-operatively led groups, especially in the fifties, were rare, it was inevitable that Rollins–the new tenor star of 1956, the virtuoso of *Worktime, Tenor Madness* and *Saxophone Colossus*–would soon leave the Max Roach Quintet and form his own group. But he had reservations about the move; again and again he regretted that a leader's extra-musical duties kept him from concentrating on the music. In strictly musical terms, too, the role of leader has not always suited him. Unlike Miles Davis or John Coltrane, he never managed during the most important years of his career to put together an ensemble that lasted more than a few months. This lack of continuity helps explains his erratic shifts in style, as well as the fact that his popularity, after a rocketlike ascent, soon lagged behind both Davis and Coltrane's.

Among musicians, Rollins was regarded as a difficult boss; there was hardly a bass player, drummer, or pianist who could meet his standards. Rollins' began his first gig as leader in November 1957 with a quintet in the Village Vanguard; he soon let Donald Byrd, the trumpeter, go, and after a series of pianists had guested, finally completed the engagement in a trio setting. The pattern is not unusual for him. (He has stated repeatedly that his preference for the trio format of sax, bass, and drums arose from his inability to find a pianist who wouldn't hem him in.) In retrospect, he says, "Years ago, I was very much like that [constantly firing musicians], when I was younger and more intense and wilder. I was really hard on my musicians–I didn't mean to be hard on them, but I wanted a musical sound, and if a guy didn't have it, I said, Well, let me try someone else. I didn't have any sentimentality about it at all–not like in my songs." (personal communication of October 18, 1987) This clear distinction–between the eminent soloist, and the paid companions whose job it is to serve his musical vision, is similarly reflected in the music. Communication between musical equals is rarely to be found in Rollins' early recordings, and is not very common in the later ones. Only on some of the records with Max Roach (like *Freedom Suite*), a few live registrations (such as Aix-en-Provence in 1959), more frequently in the early sixties–in the quartet with Don Cherry, Billy Higgins and Henry Grimes, for instance, but also in the more conservative formation with Jim Hall–

do you really get a sense that Rollins is attempting to turn his masterly monologue into a conversation. But who could really converse with him on equal terms? Jim Hall remembers: "We used to rehearse a lot, you know. But I have the feeling that the rehearsal time was mostly just to get us used to playing together...just sort of take signals from him and each other... I think, ideally, Sonny wanted it to be four-part music, and that we should react to one another, but his presence was so strong that there was no doubt who the leader was... I think Sonny liked the interplay, but also he was very much the leader." (liner notes to *The Quartets*)

Rollins himself is acutely aware of the virtuoso's isolation. "It is a very lonely position. When I started playing, the soloist was the principal person in the group. When I came up, the small groups were taking over from the big bands, and in a way it's natural for me. But it presents problems. These days it's not so much a *leader* as a *group*, and I have a problem using musicians only as an accompaniment, which is what it boils down to. Even though I don't think of them like that. They're good musicians and we want to play together–but they have to accompany me. It's a problem, and it's a bit lonely." (Cook 1985, 31) A loneliness of which the listener–and spectator–at a Rollins concert often becomes painfully aware. The allegation that Rollins ignores his players is frequent. "I've heard that comment before. I've worked with some great men in the past, but I've also worked with musicians who were not so great. In order to live with myself, I have to do what *I* feel is my best. People are coming to see me, and they expect the best performance I can give; but I must be the judge of what is best. I like to play very long introductions and endings, and that may lead people to the wrong conclusions." (Porter 1974, 14)

His insistence on determining the music's direction also explains why he has mostly declined to participate in All-Star bands—with the exception of the Milestone Jazz Stars tour of 1978. "People want to see so-called 'stars' together more... Having a group to accompany a person like me, a 'bandleader,' is now out. People are more interested in seeing VSOP or the Milestone Jazzstars… But I don't really want to do all star jobs… I would still like to have my own group, as much as possible." (Blumenthal 1982, 17)

In the eighties and nineties Rollins accomplished what he couldn't or wouldn't in previous decades: maintaining a (relatively) stable lineup, comprised of pianist Mark Soskin, trombonist Clifton Anderson, bassist Jerome Harris or Bob Cranshaw, and drummer Tommy Campbell or Marvin "Smitty" Smith; in the nineties, of Anderson, Cranshaw, Stephen Scott (piano), Jack DeJohnette or Perry Wilson (drums). Whether he has also achieved the spontaneous and equal interaction of which he speaks is still debated. The solo distribution remains uneven; Rollins may solo for as long as twenty minutes, while Clifton Anderson only rarely gets a chance to improvise—and it is always Rollins' stream of associations that determine the direction of the music. Things are not much worked out beforehand, because, as Rollins puts it: "I'm not a musician that can go to a job and do the same routine every night. Even though I might play certain songs—or a repertoire of certain songs—every night, each of these songs is going to be played differently; they're *recomposed* each time. It's one thing to have a lot of arranged-type band licks around you, which is OK; I'm not putting it down. It's something that became popular maybe in the seventies, and certainly in the eighties. But that's not where I'm coming from–I'm coming from straight improvisation, extemporaneous creativity, all of these things happening right on the spot." (Kalbacher 1988, 17) But a generational problem is evident in this ad-hoc creativity. The young musicians that Rollins plays with today cannot command the gigantic store of standards, show tunes, film music, and past hits which Rollins quotes so easily. Which means that only in his solo cadenzas can he allow his stream of consciousness free flow. In the words of trombonist Clifton Anderson, "Everyone in the band realizes that Sonny is a master, and the people turn out mainly to hear him, not us. So long as he's in a good mood and really feels like playing, we just try to keep up with him. But it can be hard. He can throw you, segueing from number to number the way he does and trying out tunes in different keys." (Davis 1986, 131)

Rollins, the group musician? Maybe it is no accident that in 1958 he already described his ultimate ambition as a concert composed for tenor saxophone and orchestra–with an unaccompanied solo... (Cerulli 1958)

the composer

"His tunes have an unusual freshness and charm, full of humor and immediately affecting." Joe Goldberg's assessment in the liner notes to *Newk's Time* (1958) could hardly be expressed

music example 9: “Pent-Up House” (beginning)

music example 10: “Oleo” (beginning)

music example 11: “Plain Jane” (beginning)

more aptly or concisely today. Rollins has committed over 100 of his own compositions to record since 1949. Some of these—"Oleo," "Doxy," "Airegin," "Pent-Up House," "St. Thomas," "Don't Stop The Carnival," "Strode Rode," "The Everywhere Calypso"—have long since become standards. And, though differing in details, these pieces share some basic traits. Most of Sonny's themes are harmonically simple, often diatonic, and just as often based on a single melodic or rhythmic idea, which is then run through in different variations. So, "Pent-Up House" plays rhythmically with the superimposition of a 3/8 motive with a binary (4/4) meter, melodically with the change from minor and major third (music example 9). "Oleo" (music example 10) explores different placement and continuation of the descending third B–G, while "Plain Jane" is based on a descending whole-tone motif almost the whole way through (music example 11). The refinement, therefore, doesn't lie in the theme but in its clever elaboration. The forms of the pieces are also refined in the details; the dependable 12- and 32-bar schemes are often honored, but just as frequently modified or abandoned. Just a few examples in outline (with the date of their first appearance on record in brackets): "The Stoppers" [1953], 24 bars, composed of four-bar segments in the formula ABABCB; "Airegin" [1954] (AB'AB" (8+12 +8+8 bars), "Strode Rode" [1956] (AABA, 8+8+4+8 bars), "Decision" (1956) (13-bar blues), "Way Out West" (1957) (20 bars).

Only on occasion has Rollins dropped the standard bebop sequence of theme–solo–theme in favor of more complex or extended patterns. The *Freedom Suite,* recorded in 1958 in a trio setting, represents the best-known exception. Here there

music example 12 (A–C): elements of the *Freedom Suite*

are four thematic blocks (marked in music example 12 as A, B, C, and D) with their own distinct musical character: theme A leads to a conventional series of solos in medium swing; B leads back to the minor and to 6/8 time. Theme C follows after a brief saxophone cadenza; it not only introduces a new key (A flat major), but a new genre (ballad). Theme D, finally, not only introduces a new tempo (up-tempo swing), but leads reprise-like back to A. The ascending fourths of the first bar of D recall the ones in the first two bars of A, while the de-

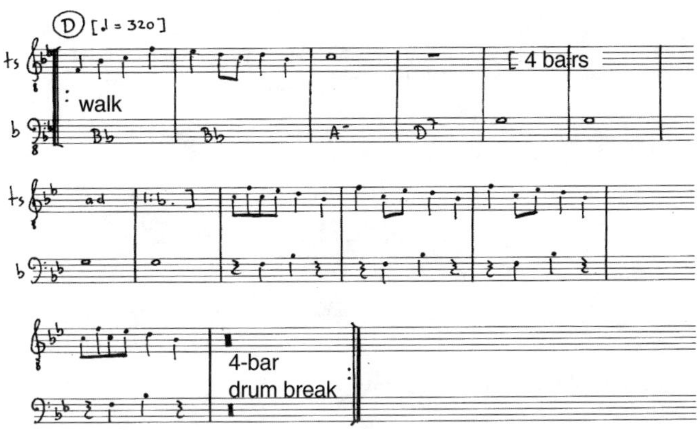

music example 12 (D): elements of the *Freedom Suite*

scending diatonic figure of bars 8–12 is a reminiscence of bars 3–4 of A–and, as if he wanted to confirm this connection, Rollins concludes The *Freedom Suite* with bars 3 and 4 of A, now transposed into the key of B flat major, the key of the D section. Not just in the wealth of themes, keys, tempos, and moods, but in the thematic linking of the opening and closing themes, *The Freedom Suite* breaks new ground. Unusual too is the way the bass and drums are integrated into the compositional scheme. The bass lines often play a central part in the composition, and the A and D sections are both shaped by a four-bar interchange between the sax and rhythm section.

Not as complex, but just as unconventional in structure is "John S." from the album *The Bridge* (1962). The piece begins with a three-part theme in 3/4 time; it is not only singularly fragmented as regards the involvement of drums and bass, but there are frequent changes of meter. A 32-bar AABA theme

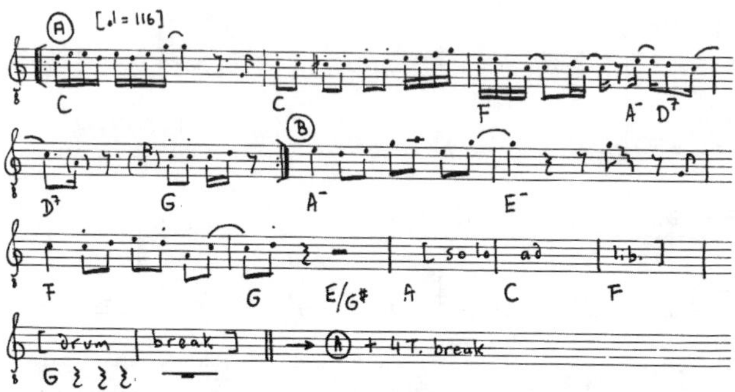

music example 13: "Joyous Lake"

follows based on the notes of the D minor triad, and introduces solos over a 34-bar chorus (18+16 bars).

The Milestone LPs of the seventies feature Rollins as an especially prolific composer. Most of the numbers he wrote himself. In the majority of cases they are simple two- or four-bar riffs, although when he composes in the fusion genre he sometimes escapes the straightjacket of 4- or 8-bar-sections. An example is "Joyous Lake" (1981) with a 9-bar B section (music example 13). In the eighties and nineties we find, alongside the fusion themes–and the calypso numbers, which, since "St. Thomas," are an essential part of his writing profile–an increasing number of themes that hark back to those of the fifties in their formal, rhythmic, and melodic character. One example is "Allison" (1987) from the LP *Dancing in the Dark.*

discography (1949–2001)

The following overview of Sonny Rollins' albums includes all the LPs/CDs he has recorded as the leader of his own ensembles at the time this book went to press. The one exception is that no attempt has been made to completely list unauthorized releases, or bootlegs. This would have been nearly impossible, given the many obscure, regional releases, which usually disappear from the market quickly. Bootlegs were generally taken into consideration only where they document groups or stylistic peculiarities for which the legal releases offer little or no help. Rollins' participation as a sideman on other musicians' albums is acknowledged in a likewise incomplete, though hopefully representative manner. This applies especially to the time between 1949 and 1957; after that, Rollins recorded almost exclusively under his own name. Various compilation albums put out by Blue Note, RCA and others, combining pieces from previously recorded LPs, have not been included.

The extensive reissue programs of the major labels have made the bulk of Sonny Rollins' oeuvre from the '50s and '60s available again–sometimes to the chagrin of the artist, who has expressed severe reservations, for example, about the issue (and subsequent CD reissue) of the *Alternative Rollins* recordings of 1964: "I feel it's my prerogative to decide how I want to be represented on records... If I don't like the way I sound, I don't want the world to hear it more than once. It's a matter of privacy almost." (McDonough 1992, 25) But, as Rollins has had to learn, a jazz icon is not granted privacy by collectors hunting down every note Rollins ever played in public. The major part of Rollins' catalog is in the possession of the Milestone, BMG, and Blue Note companies, and except for a number of Milestone recordings of the '70s and '80s (excerpts of which have been collected on the *Silver City* sampler), most of the relevant recordings are available in CD format at this writing. The following discography arranged chronologically by recording date, lists the label numbers of the original LP issues and, wherever possible, the number of the most recent CD issue. Reissues come and go, but with the help of the information provided, it should be possible to gain an overview of what's currently available and what may be a recording repackaged in a different format and/or with a different title.

J.J. Johnson / Kai Winding / Benny Green
Trombone by Three
J.J. Johnson (tb) Sonny Rollins (ts) Kenny Dorham (tp) John

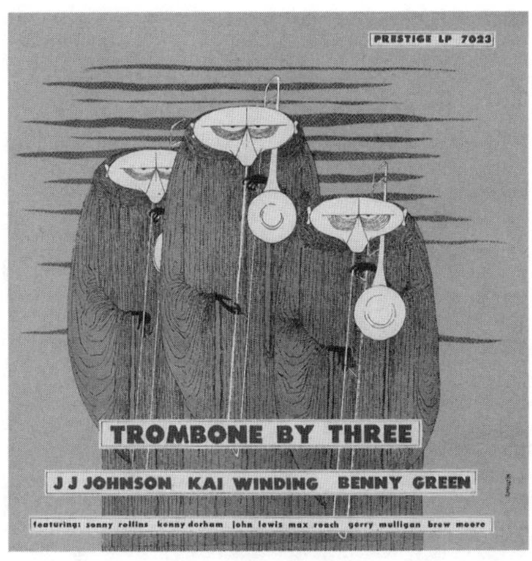

Lewis (p) Leonard Gaskin (b) Max Roach (dr); New York, 5/26/49:
ELYSEE / HI-LO / FOX HUNT / OPUS V
(Eight other tracks with different personnel, without Rollins)

This LP, a compilation of three sessions from 1949 to 1951, offers a first-class cross-section of trombone playing in the Golden Age of bebop. J.J. Johnson's sextet session offers the mixture, characteristic of bebop, of rhythm changes ("Fox Hunt"), ABA'B' forms ("Opus V") and blues ("Hi-Lo"), the last a contribution by Rollins. As a "junior partner," the 18-year-old tenor is granted less solo time than his established colleagues, but he uses it well. Typical of his playing then, Rollins combines the robust sound of the Hawkins school with Charlie Parker phraseology (especially extensive on "Hi-Lo"). In the process he introduces himself as a confident and inventive, though not yet distinctive, soloist. To the casual listener, the

combination of stylistic elements might suggest Dexter Gordon.

"Opus V," identified as a composition by J.J. Johnson, foreshadows much of the harmony and melody of the later Rollins number "Airegin." It also shares the same key (F minor). However, Johnson's theme has the standard ABA'B' structure made up of eight-bar measures, whereas in "Airegin" the first B section is extended to twelve bars.

Bud Powell
The Amazing Bud Powell, Volume 1
Blue Note CDP 7 81503 2
CD: Blue Note CDP 300 366-2
Fats Navarro (tp) Sonny Rollins (ts) Bud Powell (p) Tommy Potter (b) Roy Haynes (dr); New York, 8/8/49:
BOUNCING WITH BUD (3 takes) / WAIL (2 takes) / DANCE

OF THE INFIDELS (2 takes) / 52nd STREET THEME
(Seven additional titles with different personnel, without Rollins)

One benefit of the policy of reissuing CDs: where once you had to look for the eight takes from this session on several LPs, now they are collected on a single album in the order in which they were recorded. Since the LP version of *The Amazing Bud Powell* had different contents but the same cover, some confusion is inevitable. A word of explanation, then: The LP *The Amazing Bud Powell, Volume 1* (Blue Note 81503) contains the master takes of the four pieces. The four alternate takes can be found either on *Bud Powell: Alternate Takes* (Blue Note BST 84430) or, distributed between two LPs, on *The Fabulous Fats Navarro, Volume 1/2* (Blue Note 81531/81532), each grouped with other recordings by Powell or Navarro.

The direct comparison made possible by the multiple versions of a piece played consecutively on this CD is instructive. On the one hand, it highlights the unsteadiness in Rollins' playing–he stumbles over a phrase more than once; on the other hand, it proves (and this is the reason for those slips) that Rollins does not use a formulaic approach in his improvisations, but creates each solo individually. In this respect he differs from Navarro, who opens his improvisation in "Bouncing with Bud" three times in a row with nearly the same phrase. Of course, Rollins is still a formula-oriented soloist who always returns to a recognizable arsenal of set phrases and who has prefabricated solutions for certain harmonic situations. But his playing shows a love of experimentation that leads beyond well-worn paths. This album has particular historical value because it documents Rollins' only recorded encounter with Powell and Navarro, two great tragic figures of bop. Just eleven months after this session, the 26-year-old Navarro died of tuberculosis, aggravated by heroin addiction.

Miles Davis
Miles Davis and Horns
Prestige LP 7025 (Original Jazz Classics OJC-053)
CD: Original Jazz Classics OJCCD053-2
Miles Davis (tp) Sonny Rollins (ts) Bennie Green (tb) John Lewis (p) Percy Heath (b) Roy Haynes (dr), New York, 1/17/51:
MORPHEUS / DOWN / BLUE ROOM / WHISPERING
(Four additional titles with different personnel, without Rollins)

This January 1951 session marks both Miles Davis' premiere with the new Prestige label and the beginning of Rollins' six-year-long collaboration with the trumpeter. It is an unspectacular debut, however: four two- to three- minute pieces with competent but unremarkable solos using trite Broadway material. Only John Lewis' clever "Morpheus" arrangement, with its tempo and meter changes, stands out. "Blue Room" (which Davis interprets without the other two horns) and "Whispering" come from the '20s, and were not exactly a standard part of the bebop repertoire; but Davis and Rollins both showed a consistent preference for unusual material. Four compositions by Al Cohn, performed in February 1953 by a septet with Davis, the two tenors Cohn and Zoot Sims, and trombone player Sonny Truitt, round out the album.

Miles Davis
Down
Jazz & Jazz JJ-620
Miles Davis (tp) J.J. Johnson (tb) Sonny Rollins (ts) Kenny Drew (p) Tommy Potter (b) Art Blakey (dr); New York 6/2/51:
MOVE / HALF NELSON / DOWN
(Three additional titles with different personnel, without Rollins)

Studio productions only document one side of jazz history. One need only compare the blues "Down" from this live radio recording from Birdland with the studio version recorded a few months earlier. The studio version is calm to the point of restraint, with brief, carefully formulated solos that avoid risks. Rollins' improvisation only lasts twelve bars. But in Birdland, where the 3-minute limits of the pre-LP era no longer apply, he can take four choruses–and use them to ignite a fireworks display of double-time virtuosity. The same is true of Davis, whose artistic choruses in no way resemble the decidedly reserved lines of that January. These three pieces (which had previously been available on the bootleg market, on Ozone 7, Session 102 and Beppo 501) are important, then, in filling out and focusing our picture of the early Rollins. The idea that over the years has developed into a fixture of Rollins' reputation–that his studio recordings were but a shadow of his live performances–begins to take shape here.

On the B-side of the LP are recordings of a Miles Davis sextet with the two tenor saxophonists Eddie "Lockjaw" Davis and George "Big Nick" Nicholas, made in September 1951.

Miles Davis Featuring Sonny Rollins
Dig
Prestige LP 7012 (Original Jazz Classics-005)
CD: Original Jazz Classics OJCCD 005-2
Miles Davis (tp) Sonny Rollins (ts) Jackie McLean (as) Walter Bishop (p) Tommy Potter (b) Art Blakey (dr), New York, 10/5/51:
DIG / IT'S ONLY A PAPER MOON / DENIAL / BLUING / OUT OF THE BLUE

One can imagine that the record labels' reissue trend, so welcome to the collector, is somewhat distasteful to many musicians–there are so many old recordings they would just as soon have sink into oblivion. *Dig* is probably not one of the early works that Rollins, so liable to self-criticism, would remember fondly. The saxophonist has obvious problems with a squeaking reed on almost every track, and on "Denial" there are discrepancies in the mood that cause Rollins to stop, irritated, after just one chorus. (Later, Rollins explained to the French journalist Francois Postif: "Believe it or not, a lot of critics thought at the time that I was trying to create a new style! But who can really say where the line is that separates what you want to play, and what you actually play? I don't think that I was trying to make the reed screech... That was not one of the technical aspects of my playing... Does that satisfy you?" (Postif 1989, 77f.)

In addition, *Dig*, one of the first jazz LPs, does not make a particularly compelling argument for the positive effects on improvised music of the new long-playing format. The thematic material–aside from "It's Only a Paper Moon," a Davis original from start to finish–is thin. "Bluing" is a themeless blues, while the title of "Denial" indicates that it is another themeless variation on Parker's "Confirmation"–simply a "denial" of the "confirmation." Only "Out of the Blue" brings an original note to the adaptation of familiar structures, in that each second A section of the beloved "rhythm-changes" model of harmony is transposed a fourth higher. The most enjoyable part of this production, which seems to have been tossed off quickly, is the recorded debut of 19-year-old Jackie McLean, the only soloist who seems truly inspired.

Sonny Rollins
With the Modern Jazz Quartet
Prestige LP 7029 (Original Jazz Classics OJC-011)
CD: Original Jazz Classics OJCCD 011-2
Sonny Rollins (ts) Miles Davis (p) Percy Heath (b) Roy Haynes (dr); New York, 1/17/51:
I KNOW
Sonny Rollins (ts) Kenny Drew (p) Percy Heath (b) Art Blakey (dr); New York, 12/17/51:
TIME ON MY HANDS / MAMBO BOUNCE / THIS LOVE OF MINE / SHADRACK / SLOW BOAT TO CHINA / WITH A SONG IN MY HEART / SCOOPS / NEWK'S FADEAWAY
Sonny Rollins (ts) Milt Jackson (vib) John Lewis (p) Percy Heath (b) Kenny Clarke (dr); Hackensack NJ, 10/7/53:
IN A SENTIMENTAL MOOD / THE STOPPER / ALMOST LIKE BEING IN LOVE / NO MOE

Rollins' first LP as a leader is a patchwork, but an interesting one. "I Know" comes from the Miles Davis session in January 1951 (see *Miles Davis and Horns*). In the liner notes to the

Prestige double LP *Vintage Sessions*, a collection of early Rollins recordings, Ira Gitler recounts how the recording came about. Miles Davis, who treated the young Rollins as his protégé, had convinced Bob Weinstock, the Prestige producer, to record a feature for the tenor at the end of the studio session. Since pianist John Lewis had to report to Birdland for a show and was no longer available, Davis sat down at the piano himself and played the chords to the Charlie Parker piece "Confirmation," over which Rollins, without referring to the theme, improvised three choruses. Even though its abrupt ending betrays its impromptu origin, the solo apparently impressed Weinstock enough to offer Rollins his own studio date at the end of the year.

According to Gitler, who makes his debut as producer here, the date was not without its problems. Conga player Sabu Martinez, who was supposed to enhance "Mambo Bounce" with authentic percussive color–clearly planned with a commercial eye on the growing rumba and mambo fad–could not make it out of the Bronx because of heavy snow. While they were waiting for him, Rollins discovered that he had forgotten the shoulder strap for his saxophone. A replacement was hastily made from a wire hanger and a piece of string. As if that weren't enough, pianist Kenny Drew was so exhausted that he kept drifting off between takes.

The eight tracks that were recorded show little evidence of these problems, however. As with "I Know," Parker's spirit hovered over the music. Parker had been the first to discover the ditty "Slow Boat to China" for modern jazz. On "Mambo Bounce," a twelve-bar Rollins composition featuring saxophone and piano in a call-and-response dialogue, Rollins quotes, as his role model so often did, from Alphonse Picou's legendary "High Society" clarinet solo. Rollins' improvisations, as proficient as they are, still appear clichéd, cobbled together from current bop phrases, and they only hint at the rhythmic expertise and thematically consistent playing of later years. Rollins' preference for romantic songs (like Frank Sinatra's "This Love of Mine" and "Time on my Hands"), which he decorates with delicately interlacing motifs and not a hint of irony, is entirely personal.

For the recording date in October 1953 that justifies the title of the album, Gitler, acting once again as producer, had to begin by finding an instrument for the saxophone player, who was afflicted by drugs as usual. Otherwise, though, the session was better prepared than Prestige's usual "blowing dates." John Lewis had insisted on a separate practice session a few days before the recording, and this precaution produced good results on the two standards as well as the two Rollins tracks. The intriguing contrast between Rollins' powerful, gripping tenor sound and the cool, elegant piano phrasings of MJQ's pianist comes nicely to the fore. "No Moe" (according to Gitler, an allusion to the fact that Rollins' pianist friend Elmo Hope was nicknamed "Mo" and not "Moe") turns out to be a simple variation on "I Got Rhythm," while "The Stopper" shows Rollins' talent as a composer who creates elementary but interesting themes from simple, everyday phrases. Rollins takes three four-bar blocks of melody and puts together a 24-bar form in an ABABCB pattern.

Miles Davis
Collectors' Items

Prestige LP 7044 (Original Jazz Classics OJC-071)
CD: Original Jazz Classics OJCCD 071-2

Miles Davis (tp) Sonny Rollins, Charlie Parker (ts) Walter Bishop (p) Percy Heath (b) Philly Joe Jones (dr); New York, 1/30/53:

THE SERPENT'S TOOTH (take one) / THE SERPENT'S TOOTH (take two) / COMPULSION / 'ROUND ABOUT MIDNIGHT

Miles Davis (tp) Sonny Rollins (ts) Tommy Flanagan (p) Art Taylor (dr), Hackensack, 3/16/56:

IN YOUR OWN SWEET WAY / VIERD BLUES / NO LINE

If the third collaboration between Rollins and Davis proved disappointing, it was mainly the fault of guest star Parker, who appears on the album under the somewhat obvious pseudonym "Charlie Chan." Davis describes the situation vividly in his autobiography: "Bird had an exclusive contract with Mercury..., so he had to use a pseudonym on record. Bird had given up shooting heroin... In place of his normal big dosages of heroin, now he was drinking an enormous amount of alcohol. I remember him drinking a quart of vodka at the rehearsal, so by the time the engineer was running the tape for the session, Bird was fucked up out of his mind.

"It was like having *two* leaders at the session. Bird treated like I was his son, or a member of *his* band. But this was *my* date and so I had to get him straight... I got so angry with him that I told him off, told him that I had never done that to him on one of his recording sessions. Told him that I had always been professional on his shit. And do you know what that motherfucker said to me? He told me some shit like, 'All right, Lily Pons...to produce beauty, we must suffer pain—from the oyster comes the pearl.' He said that to me in that fucked-up, fake British accent. Then, the motherfucker fell asleep. I got so mad all over again that I started fucking up. Ira Gitler, who was producing the record for Bob Weinstock, came out of the booth and told me *I* wasn't playing shit. At this point, I was so fed up that I started packing up my horn to leave when Bird said to me, 'Miles, what are you doing?' So I told him what Ira had said, and Bird said, 'Ah, come on Miles, let's play some music.' And so we played some real good stuff after that." (Davis 1990, 151)

Some of the awkwardness of the situation is reflected in these recordings. Parker, who is heard playing tenor here for the first time since the 1947 Savoy recordings, occasionally has problems with the unfamiliar instrument, and on

"Serpent's Tooth" (like "Compulsion," a three-voiced rhythm-changes composition penned by Davis), the presentation of the theme is extremely shaky. It is interesting, though, to be able to compare the two tenors, Parker and Rollins, directly. On the same instrument, Rollins' dependence on Parker becomes obvious–even if Rollins, clearly in better shape than on the 1951 *Dig* session, at times seems to beat Parker at his own game.

The session from March 1956 seems completely relaxed, without any shadow of tragedy, even though it documents the last studio collaboration between Davis and Rollins. The two lengthy blues variations in particular ("No Line" and "Vierd Blues") show how far Rollins had come along the path of stylistic self-discovery in the last three years. He has given up bebop's stereotypical strings of eighth notes and triplets for a wonderfully free treatment of rhythm and meter, a suspenseful dramaturgy of long and short note values, and of pauses especially. "Vierd Blues" features that art of working with consistent motifs which Gunther Schuller would soon declare to be Rollins' unique contribution to jazz style.

Thelonious Monk with Sonny Rollins and Frank Foster
Monk

Prestige LP 7053 (Original Jazz Classics OJC-016)
CD: Original Jazz Classics OJCCD 016-2
Thelonious Monk (p) Sonny Rollins (ts) Julius Watkins (fr-h) Percy Heath (b) Willie Jones (dr); New York, 11/13/53:
LET'S CALL THIS / THINK OF ONE (take one) / THINK OF ONE (take two)
(Four additional titles with different personnel, without

Rollins)

Rollins' first studio encounter with the musician to whom he owed many of his artistic and personal traits–dating back to his childhood–came, of all days, on Friday the 13th. Superstition might seem justified–Ray Copeland, the trumpeter originally booked, was ill and had to be replaced at the last minute by horn player Julius Watkins, who was unfamiliar with Monk's compositions. Rollins and Monk, who had been in a car accident, arrived at the studio an hour late.

Still, the session produced worthy material. An ensemble sound as unusual as it is enjoyable is gained through the use of the French horn, which binds the unwieldy sounds of Monk and Rollins into a homogenous whole. Julius Watkins is a gem of a soloist. In "Think of One," Rollins is clearly trying to heed Monk's challenge to derive his improvisation from the theme; this is probably one of the roots of the "thematic improvisation" that became a hallmark of his solos.

The second side of the LP contains recordings of a Monk quintet with Frank Foster and Ray Copeland in May 1954.

Art Farmer
Early Art
Prestige NJLP 8258
CD: Original Jazz Classics OJCCD 680-2
Art Farmer (tp) Sonny Rollins (ts) Horace Silver (p) Percy Heath (b) Kenny Clarke (dr), Hackensack, NJ, 1/20/54:
WISTERIA / SOFT SHOE / CONFAB IN TEMPO / I'LL TAKE ROMANCE
(Other tracks with different personnel, without Rollins)

After big band engagements with Horace Henderson, Benny Carter, and finally Lionel Hampton, Art Farmer—a trumpet player who had recently moved from the West Coast to the Big Apple—got a chance to introduce himself as leader of his own combo, in the illustrious company of Prestige's renowned house musicians. The result is a high-quality, but not outstanding session with tried-and-true bop elements: standards ("I'll Take Romance"), new themes over familiar foundations ("Soft Shoe" is based on "The Lady is a Tramp," which Farmer then quotes in his solo; "Confab in Tempo," like Miles Davis' "Out of the Blue," uses the device of transposing the second A section of a rhythm-changes form up a fourth), and a ballad ("Wisteria," without Rollins). Rollins, who plays with the trumpeter in the studio for the first and last time, sails routinely through the harmonies without charting an especially original course.

Note: The four tracks listed can also be found on the Prestige double album "Farmer's Market" (Prestige P24032).

Miles Davis and the Modern Jazz Giants
Bags' Groove

Prestige LP 7109 (Original Jazz Classics OJC-245)
CD: Original Jazz Classics OJCCD 245-2

Miles Davis (tp) Sonny Rollins (ts) Horace Silver (p) Percy Heath (b) Kenny Clarke (dr); Hackensack, 6/29/54:
AIREGIN / OLEO / BUT NOT FOR ME (take two) / DOXY / BUT NOT FOR ME (take one)

This probably represents a singular achievement for a musician officially hired as a sideman: he brings three compositions to a colleague's recording session, all three are recorded, and all three immediately become jazz standards. "Airegin," "Oleo," and "Doxy" are now found in countless fake books and belong to the standard repertoire of bop amateurs worldwide. And this despite the fact that Rollins had not even finished the pieces when he brought them to the studio, as Miles Davis reports in his autobiography: "As a matter of fact, he brought the tunes in and rewrote them right in the studio. He would be tearing off a piece of paper and writing down a bar or a note or a chord, or a chord change. We'd go into a studio and I'd ask Sonny, 'Where's the tune?' And he'd say, 'I didn't write it yet,' or, 'I haven't finished it yet.' So I would play what he had and then he might go away in a corner somewhere and write shit down on scraps of paper and come back a little while after that and say, 'Okay, Miles, it's finished.' One tune he wrote was 'Oleo.' He got the title from oleomargarine, which was a big thing then, a cheap butter substitute." (Davis 1990, 169)

"Oleo" is a rhythm-changes composition with theme tones that are placed sparingly but in cunning rhythmic manner. It is further refined in that the A sections of the theme are only played by the trumpet, saxophone, and bass. Then, in the A sections of the solos, the drums are involved but not the piano—a foretaste of the pianoless ensembles Rollins would lead in the late '50s.

The up-tempo minor theme "Airegin" recalls J.J. Johnson's "Opus V" (as previously mentioned; see *Trombone by Three*). Regarding the title, Rollins says: "I saw a photograph of some Nigerian dancers in a magazine and it thrilled me very much to see. So the next song that I wrote I dedicated to the dancers, and I titled it 'Airegin,' which is Nigeria spelled backwards." (Fiofori 1971, 39)

Tracks like "Doxy" also helped establish Rollins' status as the hard-bop musician par excellence: a harmonically simple, downright old-fashioned theme in a two-beat feeling, with strong blues inflections–in short, "funky music" à la 1954.

Rollins' compositions, however, are not the only things responsible for the unprecedented success of this fourth Davis/ Rollins session (chronologically between the two included on *Collectors' Items*). The two horns are in top form, and Horace Silver's sparing, precise comping provides the perfect foil. Rollins' playing in particular radiates a supreme sense of composure. He constructs his improvisations–which have gained a noticeable rhythmic complexity compared to earlier performances–very conscientiously, with clever use of tension-building passages. As such, *Bags' Groove* represents a milestone in Rollins' recordings in every respect.

The A side of the LP offers two takes of the record's no-less legendary title track, performed by the ensemble of Miles Davis /Milt Jackson /Thelonious Monk /Percy Heath /Kenny Clarke.

Sonny Rollins
Moving Out
Prestige LP 7058 (Original Jazz Classics OJC-058)
CD: Original Jazz Classics OJCCD 058-2
Sonny Rollins (ts) Kenny Dorham (tp) Elmo Hope (p) Percy Heath (b) Art Blakey (dr), Hackensack, 8/18/54:
MOVIN' OUT / SWINGIN' FOR BUMSY / SILK 'N' SATIN / SOLID

Sonny Rollins (ts) Thelonious Monk (p) Tommy Potter (b) Arthur Taylor (dr); Hackensack, 10/25/54:
MORE THAN YOU KNOW

Sonny Rollins' second album as leader seems to have been less carefully planned than his June 1954 collaboration with Miles Davis. Although all four originals are his own, the thematic material, except for the songlike ballad "Silk 'n' Satin," falls short. "Solid" is a stereotypical blues line, and "Movin' Out" and "Swingin' for Bumsy"–adaptations of common 32-bar ABAB' or AABA forms–do not even pretend to originality through use of a new melodic superstructure. "Movin' Out" starts without a theme (which makes the carefully composed, virtuoso eight-bar unison passage for horns at the end that much more surprising); in "Swingin' for Bumsy" a riff on a single high note suffices as a starting signal. It is simply a typical blowing session, in which virtuoso up-tempo playing and a wealth of invention in a well-known framework count

for more than structural innovation. Rollins and Dorham, who plays with a robust tone and masterly phrasing, acquit themselves most eloquently in this setting, whereas Elmo Hope is occasionally thrown off track by fast tempos. In the third chorus of "Swingin' For Bumsy," he even sits out an entire A section, which his accompanists then gracefully salvage. Just as skillfully, Art Blakey conceals the fact that he forgot to bring his hi-hat cymbals to Rudy van Gelder's studio in Hackensack.

"More Than You Know" comes from the Rollins/Monk session of October 1954, whose other tracks can be found on *Thelonious Monk and Sonny Rollins.* This is yet another song from an old musical, and in his most extensive ballad interpretation to date, Rollins tries to stretch the rhythmic ties to his accompanists without severing them completely.

Thelonious Monk and Sonny Rollins
Prestige LP 7075 (Original Jazz Classics OJC-059)

CD: Original Jazz Classics OJCCD 059-2
Thelonious Monk (p) Sonny Rollins (ts) Julius Watkins (fr-h) Percy Heath (b) Willie Jones (dr); New York, 11/13/53:
FRIDAY THE THIRTEENTH
Sonny Rollins (ts) Thelonious Monk (p) Tommy Potter (b) Arthur Taylor (dr); Hackensack, 10/25/54:
THE WAY YOU LOOK TONIGHT / I WANT TO BE HAPPY

"Friday the Thirteenth" rounds out the session on *Monk* (Prestige LP-7053), and is, in a manner of speaking, the program music for that problem-ridden recording date. Both the 16-bar theme (made up of a riff repeated four times), and the improvisations are supported *ostinato* by a two-bar harmonic 'turnaround' with a melancholy descending chromatic line. For almost eleven minutes, this gives the piece a sense of something inescapably, fatefully closing in–a sense of foreboding otherwise suggested by the title. For the soloists, however, this repeated grounding provides an opportunity to explore all the harmonic and melodic implications of the two-bar sequence.

In contrast, the two tracks from October 1954 are completely cheerful. Two amiable, harmless Broadway melodies from the '20s and '30s inspire Rollins to extended, fluid, citation-rich solos that give no indication of their being a farewell performance–Rollins would be out of commission musically until November of 1955.

Clifford Brown/Max Roach
Live At the Bee Hive
Columbia JG35965
Clifford Brown (tp) Sonny Rollins, Nicky Hill (ts) Leo Blevins

(g) Billy Wallace (p) George Morrow (b) Max Roach (dr); Chicago, 11/7/55:
I'LL REMEMBER APRIL / WALKIN' / CHEROKEE / WOODY'N YOU / HOT HOUSE

"It's just a blowin' date. Just a blowin' session. Just wide open," says Max Roach in the liner notes to this double album, released by Columbia in 1979. The character of the music could not be described more aptly. For an appearance at the Bee Hive, a neighborhood bar in the South Side of Chicago, three members of the Clifford Brown/ Max Roach quintet teamed with three local musicians: Nicky Hill, Leo Blevin, and Billy Wallace. These names are not to be found in standard jazz lexicons, demonstrating once again how unfairly the official history of jazz—as documented by records and print media—is focused on the jazz scene in the Big Apple; the three Chicagoans acquit themselves quite well alongside their New York colleagues.

The fourth visitor that evening was, one might say, a New Yorker in exile: Sonny Rollins. He plays here for the first time with the Brown/Roach combo, and in public for the first time since his self-enforced hiatus. No dramatic change of style is revealed on these recordings. The listener's ears do prick up, however, at several spots on "Walkin' " and "Hot House," where Rollins experiments with a rhythmic and melodically fragmented style of playing.

The outstanding musician in this lengthy jam session, with its sometimes half-hour-long pieces, is Clifford Brown, who impresses with his overflowing ideas, his dazzling proficiency and his consistently round tone, full and warm in every register; his playing is the best thing preserved from this private live recording. Otherwise, distortions, interruptions, and harmony instruments barely audible over long stretches detract significantly from one's pleasure. In addition, the two last tracks are only partly recorded, while "I'll Remember April" is interrupted by a pause probably caused by a tape change. Max Roach explains why the recordings had to wait almost a quarter-century to be released: "The only thing that survived the crash was this tape. I cherished this tape all those years... I would take it out when Dizzy would come to the house, or trumpet players like Jimmy Owens. But I never played it that much. It hurt me to play it."

Sonny Rollins
Worktime
Prestige LP 7020 (Original Jazz Classics OJC-007)
CD: Original Jazz Classics OJCCD 007-2
Sonny Rollins (ts) Ray Bryant (p) George Morrow (b) Max Roach (dr); Hackensack, 12/2/55:
THERE'S NO BUSINESS LIKE SHOW BUSINESS / PARADOX / RAINCHECK / THERE ARE SUCH THINGS / IT'S ALL RIGHT WITH ME

"Okay, fellas"—Rollins' hoarse voice is heard in the background, and together with Max Roach's intro to "There's No Business Like Show Business," it kicks off one of Rollins' most brilliant sessions. In the opinion of many of the saxophone player's fans it is the equal of the epochal *Saxophone Colossus* recordings. "There's No Business..." is another example of Rollins' taste in unusual, some might say frivolous, themes, supposedly unsuited to jazz. Does Rollins wish to satirize Irving

Berlin's melody? The moody downward glissandos in his introduction to the theme might suggest as much. Perhaps, however, he is just drawn to the unusual 48-bar form, composed of eight-bar A- and 16-bar B-sections in an ABA'B' pattern. Many soloists would have difficulties with the murderous tempo of 1/4 = 370, or just give up and do simple finger exercises, but not Rollins. More than that, he constructs choruses–out of breathtakingly long phrases of eighth-note chains, unexpected rests and repeatedly interspersed fragments of the theme–that achieve a unique balance of discontinuity (that is, unexpectedness) and inner coherence. The ballad "There Are Such Things" also comes alive through this manner of improvising that wanders far afield but always returns to the melody. Here, too, as on the rest of *Worktime*, Rollins' virtuosity does not begin with the first solo chorus, but is already evident in the exceptionally nuanced presentation of the theme. Considering the highly individual take on familiar tunes, it is hardly a cause for regret that only one original is represented–"Paradox," an AABA theme with Latin-tinged A-sections.

Important contributions to the outstanding whole are made both by bassist George Morrow, with a firm beat and wonderfully round tone, and Max Roach, the personification of the intelligent drummer, with his variegated timekeeping as well as his superior solos. On "Paradox" and "Raincheck" Roach holds forth with Rollins in four- and eight-bar exchanges without bass or piano. Rudy van Gelder's excellent sound equipment contributes its share to make *Worktime*, Rollins' return to the jazz scene, a signal triumph.

Clifford Brown and Max Roach
At Basin Street
EmArcy MG 36070
Clifford Brown (tp) Sonny Rollins (ts) Richie Powell (p, celesta on "Time") George Morrow (b) Max Roach (dr); New York, 1/4/56:
GERTRUDE'S BOUNCE / POWELL'S PRANCES
Same personnel, 2/16/56:
WHAT IS THIS THING CALLED LOVE / LOVE IS A MANY-SPLENDORED THING
Same personnel, 2/17/56:
I'LL REMEMBER APRIL / TIME / THE SCENE IS CLEAN

Basin Street was the name of the jazz club on the corner of Broadway and 51st Street which in the '50s hosted big names like Erroll Garner, Buck Clayton, and the Brown–Roach quintet. Despite the name, however, which suggests a live setting, this EmArcy LP was recorded in three studio sessions.

The music has a completely different character from the *Live at the Bee Hive* recordings: instead of an unrestrained blowing session, we have a carefully prepared studio date with mainly short solos. Pianist Richie Powell's composing skills are especially featured. As a soloist, he always stood in the shadow of his brother Bud (whose "Un Poco Loco" he quotes in his solo in "I'll Remember April"), and in this formation he can hardly hold his own in improvisations alongside the young giants Brown and Rollins. As a composer and arranger, however, he makes essential contributions to the quintet's tight ensemble sound. Three of the tracks included here ("Powell's Prances," "Time," and "Gertrude's Bounce") come from his pen, and he knows how to rejuvenate even overworked standards with original intros and arrangements. This applies especially to the movie theme "Love is a Many-Splendored Thing"–which is normally fairly shallow–but which Powell transforms into a chamber-music-like showpiece with unusual meters (5/4 time), polyrhythmic layerings, and sudden rhythm changes.

With the structural ideas of Powell, the virtuoso solos of Brown and Rollins, and the rhythmical fire of Morrow and Roach, all the ingredients for high-quality hard bop are accounted for. Also, more clearly than on the sonically inferior *Live at the Bee Hive* recordings, the captivating contrast between Brown's elegant, round tone and Rollins' bristly tenor sound comes to the fore.

Clifford Brown/Max Roach
Pure Genius (Volume One)
Elektra Musician MUS K 52 388
Clifford Brown (tp) Sonny Rollins (ts) Richard Powell (p)

George Morrow (b) Max Roach (dr); location unknown, beginning of 1956:
WHAT'S NEW / I'LL REMEMBER APRIL / DAAHOUD / LOVER MAN / 52ND STREET THEME

The tapes that are the basis of this release come from the collection of Clifford Brown's widow, LaRue Brown-Watson. The record quality, as is to be expected of amateur recordings from this time, is mediocre and uneven (which suggests that the tapes come from different concerts), but overall better than the *Bee Hive* recordings. Apart from Brown's "Daahoud," the repertoire is made up of popular pieces of the time–showcases for the horns' long solo excursions, little more. While Rollins does not get past a competent paraphrasing of the harmonies in "Daahoud," in "I'll Remember April" he plays masterfully with the rhythmic base, letting razor-sharp chains of eighth-notes alternate with extended phrases that float freely above the beat. On the "52nd Street Theme," however, it is hard to decide whether Rollins' fragmented solo is an expression of an unconventional idea or rather a result of the breakneck tempo of 420 bpm, where the pianist, for his part, is clearly overextended.

"*Volume One*" suggests that Elektra intended to release other volumes from this source; since this record has been long out of print, it looks like the erratic record market has put those plans on hold.

Sonny Rollins Plus 4
Prestige LP 7038 (Original Jazz Classics OJC-243)
CD: Original Jazz Classics OJCCD 243-2
Sonny Rollins (ts) Clifford Brown (tp) Richie Powell (p) George

Morrow (b) Max Roach (dr); Hackensack, 3/22/56:
I FEEL A SONG COMING ON / PENT-UP HOUSE / VALSE HOT / KISS AND RUN / COUNT YOUR BLESSINGS

The neutrally named combo *Sonny Rollins Plus 4* turns out to be none other than the Clifford Brown–Max Roach quintet, known from the previous records. Still, the *ad hoc* name was more than a legality (the quintet was under contract to Mercury); Rollins does set the tone here. The three seldom-played Broadway melodies undoubtedly come from the thick pile of music he reportedly carried around in his saxophone case at all times. "Valse Hot" and "Pent-Up House" are two Rollins themes that, like "Doxy," "Oleo," and "Airegin," became instant standards. Rollins' waltz–possibly the first successful jazz waltz since Fats Waller's "Jitterbug Waltz"–is sustained by the freedom in which the simple, melodic motifs are set against the form and rhythm of the 16-bar piece. "Pent-Up House," too, depends on some sleight of hand: the charm of the four-bar phrase representing the entire theme lies in the tension between a binary meter and a melody that is organized in triple-time phrases—an old trick, admittedly, and familiar since Glenn Miller's "In the Mood," but still effective.

Did Rollins once again write down the themes in the studio? Clifford Brown's uncharacteristic fluffs in the presentation of the theme at the beginning and end of "Valse Hot" suggest that he was seeing the tune for the first time; and other moments in the recording feed the suspicion that this was a hastily produced—though ultimately rewarding—session.

Sonny Rollins
Tenor Madness
Prestige LP 7074 (Original Jazz Classics OJC-124)
CD: Original Jazz Classics OJCCD 124-2
Sonny Rollins (ts) John Coltrane (ts, only on "Tenor Madness") Red Garland (p) Paul Chambers (b) Philly Joe Jones (dr); Hackensack, 5/24/56:
MY REVERIE / THE MOST BEAUTIFUL GIRL IN THE WORLD / PAUL'S PAL / WHEN YOUR LOVER HAS GONE / TENOR MADNESS

One of the most famous combo recordings of the 1950s came about by chance. When, on May 24, 1956 Sonny Rollins had a recording date in Rudy van Gelder's studio in Hackensack, John Coltrane stopped by, possibly just to visit with his three colleagues from the Miles Davis quintet. What could be more natural at the end of the session than essaying a tenor dialogue based on the universal blues in B flat? The word "dialogue" is chosen deliberately. "Tenor Madness" is not one of the popular tenor battles of the day. There is little here in the way of competition or striving to outdo the other. Rather, it is a very respectful but substantial conversation between two distinctly different saxophone personalities. Their styles become clear in the extended solos after the rifflike opening theme: Coltrane immediately goes into a hectic double-time in the first of his seven choruses without really finding an overall direction. Again and again his choruses begin with clear phrases, only to fray into somewhat dull runs and perfunctory sequences. The rushed, strained impression he makes is reinforced by his thin, pinched tone. Not so with Rollins. He approaches his solo in a relaxed way, with simple phrases that gradually merge into longer lines. Only at the end of his eighth and final chorus does he use a double-time run as a final crescendo that is that much more arresting. His sound continues to be round and warm, and unlike Coltrane, who hardly uses the instrument's lowest octave, Rollins prefers the middle and lower registers. In this regard, *Tenor Madness* is an impressive demonstration of two differing approaches to the blues, and to saxophone playing in general. The saxophone dialogue comes only after piano and bass solos and four-bar exchanges with the drums. For twelve choruses, the two tenors switch off in four-bar phrases, and these fours, so often just a stereotypical exercise at the end of hard-bop numbers, turn into a brilliant display of musical interaction. Coltrane opens the conversation, then Rollins takes up his melodic, harmonic and technical ideas—it is as though two voices

with defined roles were reciting a text they knew equally well. Rollins only occasionally chooses contrast over imitation or variation; then, instead of elaborating Coltrane's breathless arabesques, he echoes them, almost ironically, with markedly calm mirror images. In this way the thirteen minutes of "Tenor Madness" turns into a clinic on saxophone stylistics in '50s jazz.

The other four tracks are less interesting. Rollins chose three especially friendly and catchy themes from his rich repertoire of Broadway material, paraphrasing them with an unusually soft sound. His improvisations radiate a sense of relaxation, and in "My Reverie" he approximates Ben Webster's ballad romanticism with a breathy subtone and pronounced vibrato. Even Rollins' own composition "Paul's Pal," a minor theme in the familiar AABA form in which saxophone and drum ac-

cents melt into a dreamy synchronicity, fits the mood, and Red Garland's elegant, sparkling piano is made to order. Paul Chambers shifts to the frontline as a third soloist, with bravura *pizzicato* and *arco* improvisations.

Sonny Rollins
Saxophone Colossus
Prestige LP 7079 (Original Jazz Classics 291)
CD: Original Jazz Classics OJCCD 291-2
Sonny Rollins (ts) Tommy Flanagan (p) Doug Watkins (b) Max Roach (dr); Hackensack, 6/22/56:
YOU DON'T KNOW WHAT LOVE IS / ST. THOMAS / STRODE RODE / BLUE SEVEN / MORITAT

Less than a month after *Tenor Madness* comes another milestone of the Rollins discography, a recording repeatedly cited as Rollins' *chef d'oeuvre*, and one of the classic jazz albums of all time. Not that *Saxophone Colossus* represents anything radically new in Rollins' playing; but it shows to best effect elements of Rollins' style that had previously been dispersed among miscellaneous recordings and compositions. So, for instance, there is his penchant for unconventional material–represented in this case by "Moritat" (better known as "Mack the Knife" from Brecht and Weill's *Threepenny Opera*); his talent for inventing melodies that are accessible, but have unconventional details–like "Strode Rode", a song in AABA form with a 12-bar A, and four-bar B section. There is his mastery in the handling of ballads–here represented by "You Don't Know What Love Is," where the statement of the theme already impresses, and even more so the solo, which hovers between rubato and strict adherence to the meter, moves through various tempos, and explores the tenor's full range, down to the resonant low B flat.

Saxophone Colossus achieved lasting fame in large part because of "Blue Seven," a carefully constructed blues with a theme that draws unmistakably on "Vierd Blues" from March of the same year. It inspired Gunther Schuller to write his much-cited analysis that appeared in 1958 in *Jazz Review*, hailing Rollins as the "central figure of this present renewal" of jazz (Schuller 1986, 86; Schuller's article is discussed in the stylistic chapter above).

But new facets of Rollins' wide-ranging musicianship are revealed also; with "St. Thomas" (named after one of the Virgin Islands), Rollins proclaims his West Indian roots for the first time–and contributes another item to the catalog of classic jazz melodies. The light-footed, carefree tone of the piece should not overshadow the fact that Rollins' improvisation

here is even more thematically oriented than on the highly praised "Blue Seven." The sparkling precision and structural intelligence of Max Roach's drumming and the resonant beat of Doug Watkins' bass ably support the saxophonist's flights of fancy.

Sonny Rollins Quintet
Rollins Plays for Bird
Prestige LP 7095 (Original Jazz Classics OJC-214)
CD: Original Jazz Classics OJCCD 214-2
Sonny Rollins (ts) Kenny Dorham (tp) Wade Legge (p) George Morrow (b) Max Roach (dr); Hackensack, 10/5/56:
MEDLEY: I REMEMBER YOU / MY MELANCHOLY BABY / OLD FOLKS / THEY CAN'T TAKE THAT AWAY FROM ME / JUST FRIENDS / MY LITTLE SUEDE SHOES / STAR EYES / KIDS KNOW / I'VE GROWN ACCUSTOMED TO YOUR FACE

When the "most important saxophonist to carry on and enrich the Parker tradition" (Ira Gitler, on the cover) and two prominent Parker sidemen (Dorham and Roach) unite to pay a musical tribute to the late bebop genius, expectations run high. Disappointment is that much greater when the results fall short. Although the medley dedicated to Parker begins with the introductory figure of "Parker's Mood," what follows are not the bop hero's compositions but merely pieces that Parker liked to play in his later years. Even that would be no cause for complaint, if only the series of melodies were not offered up with such want of energy and originality. All seven pieces are played in the same medium tempo, and all but the last follow the stereotypical arrangement of a solo chorus, a half chorus of fours from the soloist and the drummer, and a half chorus of the theme to close. More or less inspired piano passages bridge the segments of the medley. The B side of the album strengthens the impression that, for the Sonny Rollins quintet (which, after the death of Clifford Brown and Richie Powell, is identical with the new Max Roach quintet), this was not an especially good day. Rollins' "Kids Know" is a fairly original theme in 3/4 time, but is stretched out to almost 12 minutes, which seems even longer because the rhythm section sounds uninspired, and practically drags. "I've Grown Accustomed To Your Face" (from *My Fair Lady*) is a nice, but hardly exceptional ballad feature for Rollins.

Max Roach + 4
EmArcy MG 36098
CD: EmArcy 822 673-2
Kenny Dorham (tp) Sonny Rollins (ts) Ray Bryant (p) Max Roach (dr, perc) George Morrow (b); New York, 10/12/56:

EZZ-THETIC / DR. FREE-ZEE / JUST ONE OF THOSE THINGS / MR. X / BODY AND SOUL / WOODY'N YOU

Although Stuart Nicholson suggests in an article in *The Wire* that Rollins' "laid-back, almost lackluster solos" in the October 5th *Plays For Bird* recordings was a psychological consequence of Clifford Brown's tragic death nearly three months earlier (Nicholson 1985), his hypothesis is challenged by the present recordings, made only a week later. The newly formed Max Roach quintet's makes an extremely vital recording debut, in no way feeble or depressed.

Of course Kenny Dorham has a hard time filling Brown's shoes; unlike Dorham, Brown would probably not have struggled with the breakneck tempo of "Just One of Those Things." Still, Dorham is a fine, only slightly less spectacular trumpet player whose dark timbre and elegant, careful phrasing harmonize wonderfully with Rollins' aggressive tenor.

What has changed is not just the ensemble, but the repertoire. "Ezz-thetic" is an intriguingly unwieldy and too seldom-played theme by George Russell, the theoretician who came up with the Lydian chromatic concept. Oddly enough, it inspires Rollins, in the bridge of his second solo chorus, to break free of the beat into some freestyle "sheets of sound" playing à la Coltrane. Roach contributes two compositions of his own. The blues "Free-Zee" is a feature for his highly distinctive artistry on the cymbals, snare, and kettledrum (most likely added in an overdub), and provides striking evidence that thematic improvisation is not the sole privilege of the so-called melody instruments. "Mr. X" is suggestive of Rollins' "Airegin." The outstandingly balanced, transparent sound of this 1956 EmArcy recording would stand up alongside recent recordings of our high-tech era.

Thelonious Monk
Brilliant Corners
Riverside RLP 12-226 (Original Jazz Classics OJC-026)
CD: Original Jazz Classics OJCCD 026-2
Thelonious Monk (p, celesta on "Pannonica") Ernie Henry (as) Sonny Rollins (ts) Oscar Pettiford (b); New York, 10/9/56:
BA-LUE-BOLIVAR BA-LUES-ARE / PANNONICA
Same personnel; New York, 10/15/56:
BRILLIANT CORNERS
Thelonious Monk (p) Clark Terry (tp) Sonny Rollins (ts) Paul Chambers (b) Max Roach (dr, perc); New York, 12/7/56:
BEMSHA SWING
Thelonious Monk (p), same date and location:
I SURRENDER DEAR

Several anecdotes circulate concerning the personal and musical problems experienced during the recording of Monk's composition "Brilliant Corners." It seems that this talented quintet was unable to produce a single take acceptable from start to finish; the version that was released is an artifact pieced together in the editing room. The musicians' difficulties are understandable; "Brilliant Corners" is a piece with awkward motifs, unusual advances in harmony, and a completely bizarre form. An eight-bar A section is followed by a seven-bar B section, which is succeeded by another seven-bar version of A; the whole theme is then repeated in double time, but now with the regular eight-bar A conclusion. In addition, this structure is the basis for not only the theme, but also the improvisations. The rhythm section's occasional missteps can be heard on the bridges between segments; Sonny Rollins and Ernie Henry, on the other hand, are able to master the form and produce coherent lines that make that connection between theme and solo that Monk so often encouraged. The mosaic that Monk had unconventionally put together from the elements of bebop syntax is taken apart here, and the fragments no less unconventionally recombined. Monk, Rollins, and the brilliant and short-lived Henry—three musicians with forceful, unmistakable styles, who manage to avoid the pitfalls of bebop clichés—give the frontline a uniquely sharp and individual sound.

It is clear on the other tracks, too, how close Rollins' musical ideas come to Monk's, now that Rollins has rid himself of his Parker habits. Both Rollins and Monk are virtuosos of the dramatics of notes and rests, masters of dissecting thematic material in their improvisations. But while Monk generally explores the discontinuity of different aspects of the theme and leaves it at that, Rollins often takes off from a fragment and weaves it into increasingly longer lines. For example, in "Ba-Lue Bolivar Ba-Lues-Are" (named after the Bolivar Hotel in New York), he takes up *verbatim* the closing phrase of Monk's solo, beginning sparingly with many pauses, to gradually build a continuous sequence of double-time phrases in a grand arc spanning several choruses.

With four now-classic Monk melodies, an outstanding ensemble, and plenty of surprising touches (like Monk's celesta playing on "Pannonica" and Roach's kettledrum roll on "Bemsha Swing"), *Brilliant Corners* represents the high point of Monk and Rollins' collaboration. This makes it the more regrettable that this would be their last full-scale recording together—Monk makes only a brief appearance (limited to two tracks) on the Blue Note LP *Sonny Rollins Vol. 2* in April of the following year.

Sonny Rollins
Tour De Force
Prestige LP 7126 (Original Jazz Classics OJC-095)
CD: Original Jazz Classics OJCCD 095-2
Sonny Rollins (ts) Kenny Drew (p) George Morrow (b) Max Roach (dr) Earl Coleman (voc on "Two Different Worlds" and "My Ideal"); Hackensack, 12/7/56:
EE-AH / B. QUICK / TWO DIFFERENT WORLDS / B. SWIFT / MY IDEAL

Sonny Rollins
Sonny Boy
Prestige LP 7207 (Original Jazz Classics OJC-348)
Personnel, date and location same as preceding:
EE-AH / B. QUICK / B. SWIFT / SONNY BOY
Sonny Rollins (ts) Kenny Dorham (tp) Wade Legge (p) George Morrow (b) Max Roach (dr); Hackensack, 10/5/56:
THE HOUSE I LIVE IN

Down Beat critic Dick Hadlock accused the Sonny Rollins of the late fifties of an "I'm the new Bird" attitude (Hadlock 1962). Listening to *Tour De Force,* one might agree. The saxophone player here is mainly interested in demonstrating his musical, or, rather, his instrumental, technique. "B. Quick" has to be one of the fastest recordings in jazz history. At the almost superhuman speed of 450 bpm and with a crystal-clear timbre, Rollins races through the harmonies of "Cherokee," naturally prompting comparison with Parker's legendary "Cherokee" adaptation "Koko," which at a speed of 310 bpm seems comparatively laid-back. When Rollins plays runs of eighth notes at this tempo (which he does most of the time), he is

playing fifteen notes a second, reaching the limits of the physically possible. Many of his phrases seem, unlike Parker's, to be slurred and imprecise. Because of this, "B. Quick" impresses one as more an athletic than a musical achievement, and hence provoked Hadlock's charge of showing off. The same thing goes for the only slightly slower "B. Swift," which for its part is based on the chord progression of "Lover" (again without a theme). (On both steeplechases, only Max Roach succeeds in keeping pace with Rollins without evident strain.) The blues "Ee-Ah" is musically more compelling because it is less breathless and its motifs more coherent. Rollins takes off from a simple riff, a reference point to which he always returns after his virtuoso arabesques. *Tour De Force* is a record of the greatest possible contrasts. In the romantic ballads "Two Different Worlds" and "My Ideal," we are treated to Earl Coleman's sonorous baritone voice, with its warm vibrato, occasionally interspersed with pathetic sobs. "Sonny is in love," explains

Max Roach of these surprisingly sentimental guest vocals, which Rollins garnishes with delicate variations on the theme. Or was the ghost of Parker, the musical godfather, hovering over the session? Earl Coleman, after all, had achieved fame with his interpretations of "Dark Shadows" and "This is Always," which he recorded with the bebop genius in 1947…

The LP *Sonny Boy* was awkwardly compiled from musical leftovers, for commercial reasons. It came onto the market in 1961, when Rollins had been absent from the scene almost two years, and his fan base was thirsting for new releases. Prestige producer Bob Weinstock dug through his archives and found, in a box marked "Extras," two unreleased tracks from the *Tour De Force* and *Plays For Bird* sessions of 1956. Since this was not enough for an LP, the instrumental tracks from *Tour De Force* were added, avoiding the combination of aggression and romantic pathos that had irritated some on *Tour De Force.* It should be noted, however, that this contrast attracted others to the original *Tour De Force* LP, and in the end simply reflects the contrasts in Rollins' personality.

Sonny Rollins

Blue Note BLP 1542 (Blue Note BST 81542)
CD: Blue Note CDP 7 815422
Sonny Rollins (ts) Donald Byrd (tp) Wynton Kelly (p) Gene Ramey (b) Max Roach (dr); Hackensack, 12/16/56:
DECISION / BLUESNOTE / HOW ARE THINGS IN GLOCCA MORRA / PLAIN JANE / SONNYSPHERE

Did Rollins try to appear ultra-conventional for his debut on the august Blue Note label? The repertoire for this LP certainly seems straight out of the hard-bop manual: two blues tracks, two 32-bar AABA forms, one ballad. In fact some things on this record do seem schematic, clichéd, and perfunctory (like many of the Blue Note LPs that came out in the late fifties). "Sonnysphere" uses a casually tossed off, common riff as an excuse to work over the chords of "I Got Rhythm," and "Bluesnote" is—how could it be otherwise?—a blues in B flat, of whose theme Rollins composed only the first four and the last two bars.

But the details surprise. "Plain Jane"—like "Oleo"—is an exercise in rhythmic complication within the familiar AABA frame; the beat is unpredictably displaced and the intervals of the simple motif altered. Subtler still is "Decision," a 13-bar (!) blues with a brief, recurring motif of repeated notes, which Rollins subjects to many improvisational variations. By comparison, the schmaltzy "How Are Things in Glocka Morra" seems completely trite at first; but then one notices that it has a quite unusual AA'B form with segments of eight, ten, and twelve bars respectively. And Rollins' way of subtly paraphrasing and interpreting popular melodies is always worth hearing.

The trumpet player Donald Byrd, who became famous through an engagement with Art Blakey's Jazz Messengers, contributes thoughtful solos without, however, justifying his reputation as Clifford Brown's successor. To be fair, next to Rollins—with his rich palette of tone colors, from the harsh staccato of "Bluesnote" to the velvety legato of "Glocka Morra"—every other horn player pales by comparison.

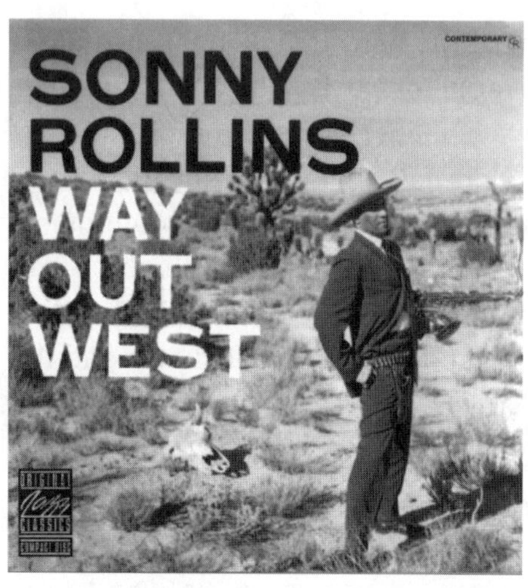

Sonny Rollins
Way Out West
Contemporary C 3530/S 7530 (Original Jazz Classics OJC-337)
CD: Original Jazz Classics OJCCD 337-2
Sonny Rollins (ts) Ray Brown (b) Shelly Manne (dr); Los Angeles, 3/7/57:
I'M AN OLD COWHAND / SOLITUDE / COME, GONE / WAGON WHEELS / THERE IS NO GREATER LOVE / WAY OUT WEST

Way Out West inaugurated a series of great trio recordings that continued through March of 1959. The idea of a jazz combo without harmony instruments was not new. Gerry Mulligan had realized it at the beginning of the decade in his celebrated quartet recordings with Chet Baker. But there the counterpoint of the two wind instruments supported the soloist, making the harmonies clear. Rollins has no such support in the *Way Out West* recordings, and probably consciously decided against it; bad experiences with pianists, whose busy playing crowded his improvisations, made the pianoless ensemble seem more like a liberation than a sacrifice. And unlike Mulligan, whose pianoless recordings were short and carefully arranged, Rollins uses his newfound freedom for lengthy solo excursions in which the rhythmic and harmonic potential of the themes is taken to the limit. The thematic elements are randomly moved around, the four- or eight-bar phrases are stretched like rubber bands, the harmonic changes are arbitrarily anticipated or postponed. *Way Out West* is tense and suspenseful music—and humorous besides. Rollins' improvisational boldness contrasts almost grotesquely with the banality of the cowboy songs "Wagon Wheels" and "I'm An Old Cowhand," where the Western flavor is enhanced by Shelly Manne's imitation of hoofbeats. This was Rollins' way of musically celebrating his first trip to the West Coast; the LP cover (designed by Rollins), showing the young saxophone hero with a Stetson hat, holster and "weapon" at the ready, is the optical complement to this musical irony. It is obvious that Rollins greatly enjoyed reflecting the childhood impressions of countless cowboy films in his music. The other tracks also come alive with this evident joy in playing. In this way, the themeless "Come, Gone," built on familiar harmonic sequences, becomes a virtuoso paraphrasing of rhythm-and-blues riffs. The unusual recording hour—because of the three virtuosos' time commitments, the session began at three in the morning—seems to have been more inspiring than fatiguing.

In the trio setting, each musician is pitilessly exposed, and Rollins' daring solo digressions call for a rock-solid foundation. Ray Brown's rhythmically stable, harmonically unique, and melodically catchy bass, combined with Shelly Manne's metronomic but lively, responsive and colorful percussion, ensure that Rollins' gambles pay off. Admittedly, the kind of discursive interplay later pioneered by Bill Evans' 1961 trio, which set standards for chamber-music-like communication within jazz combos, is not to be found here. Each musician's role is well defined, and hardly ever called into question.

Max Roach
Jazz in 3/4 Time
EmArcy MG 36108
Kenny Dorham (tp) Sonny Rollins (ts) Ray Bryant (p) George Morrow (b) Max Roach (dr); New York, 10/12/56:
THE MOST BEAUTIFUL GIRL IN THE WORLD
Same personnel, except Billy Wallace replaces Ray Bryant; New York 3/18–21/57:
BLUES WALTZ / VALSE HOT / I'LL TAKE ROMANCE / LITTLE FOLKS / LOVER

Sonny Rollins' last recording as a member of the Max Roach quintet originated with an idea by producer Bob Shad. Inspired, perhaps, by the success of Rollins' "Valse Hot," he had proposed an album of jazz waltzes. "Jazz musicians play everything in 4/4 time," Roach observes on the record cover– even pieces like "I'll Take Romance," "Lover," or "The Most Beautiful Girl In The World" that were originally composed in 3/4 time. (As if to substantiate his theory, only months earlier, on *Tenor Madness,* Rollins had served up a 4/4 version of the last piece.)

Concept albums often come across as contrived. This one is no different. Of course, musicians of this caliber can produce evidence that even a waltz can swing, and had done so before. But after more than forty minutes of uninterrupted 3/4 meter one is apt to feel that the jazz waltz should be the exception rather than the rule.

"The Most Beautiful Girl In The World" is a relic of the *Max Roach + 4* session of October 1956. Two things differentiate the older and more recent parts of the album. The sound quality of the five newer tracks is much worse–duller, less transparent. One advantage, however, is the participation of pianist Billy Wallace (first encountered in the *Bee Hive* session of November 1955), who is inventive both in solos and accompaniment. In "Valse Hot" his right and left hands engage in eloquent dialogues, that culminate–unusually for jazz piano–in genuine counterpoint. On "I'll Take Romance" he impresses with his virtuoso phrases in parallel octaves.

Sonny Rollins
Vol. 2

Blue Note BLP 1558 (BST 81558)
CD: Blue Note CDP 497 809-2

Sonny Rollins (ts) J. J. Johnson (tb) Horace Silver (p except on "Reflections") Thelonious Monk (p, only on "Misterioso" and "Reflections") Paul Chambers (b) Art Blakey (dr); Hackensack, 4/14/57:

WHY DON'T I? / YOU STEPPED OUT OF A DREAM / POOR BUTTERFLY / WAIL MARCH / MISTERIOSO / REFLECTIONS

This record would be a routine matter—hard bop in the tried-and-true Blue-Note format, with first-class musicians but without any particular thematic or improvisational highlights—were it not for two tracks by Rollins' mentor Thelonious Monk. In the first place, he contributes the most interesting pieces: the blues "Misterioso," which proceeds in a rigid (that is, nonswinging) eighth-note rhythm and in equally uniform intervals of sixths. The other piece is the sensitive ballad "Reflections," which inspires Rollins to create a masterwork of thematic improvisation.

Secondly, Monk makes "Misterioso," in which he alternates at the piano with Horace Silver, a fascinating demonstration of different pianistic styles. While Silver uses the basic blues harmonies as a foil for typical funk clichés of the time, Monk plays with the mosaic tiles of the theme with characteristic persistence and ingenuity.

Kenny Dorham
Jazz Contrasts
Riverside RLP 12-239 (Original Jazz Classics OJC-028)
Kenny Dorham (tp) Sonny Rollins (ts [not on "Larue" and "But Beautiful"]) Hank Jones (p) Betty Glamman (harp, only on "Larue," "My Old Flame," and "But Beautiful") Oscar Pettiford (b) Max Roach (dr); New York 5/21, 27/1957:
FALLING IN LOVE WITH LOVE / I'LL REMEMBER APRIL / LARUE / MY OLD FLAME / BUT BEAUTIFUL / LA VILLA

Two Kenny Dorhams gaze out at the observer from the record cover, one carefree and informal, shirt open at the neck, the other serious and formal, in jacket and tie. The musical counterpart to this is the contrast between relaxed medium- and up-tempo pieces and carefully arranged ballads, whose seriousness is underscored by the addition of a harp. This brings preconceptions about "popular" and "serious" music right to the forefront.

As one might expect, the music gains little substance from the classically glorified harp. Although the harp chords complement Hank Jones' dry comping surprisingly well–often, the piano and harp meld into a kind of super string instrument–the inevitable harp glissandos and arpeggios are superfluous and confirm one's suspicions that the instrument is a needless extravagance.

Rollins is mainly heard on the (faster, less arranged) harpless tracks, which contain almost no musical surprises. Here, the three dominant personalities of the Max Roach quintet (which had just been dissolved) play the music already familiar from the previous Roach and Rollins records. This is especially true

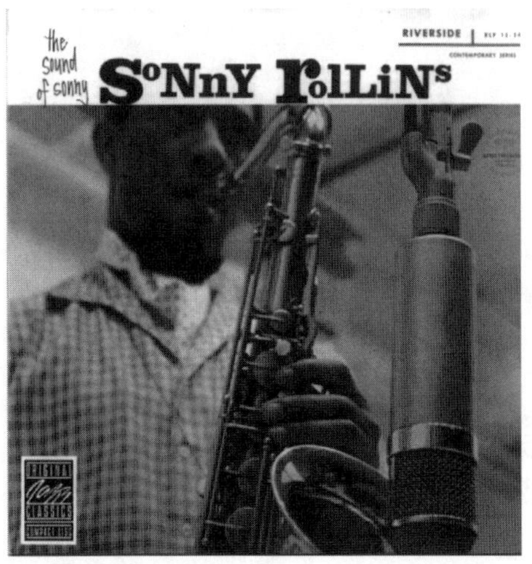

of the furious, almost pretentiously fast "I'll Remember April," where Rollins' rhythmic finesse stands out.

The recording quality of this Riverside record is noticeably inferior to that of the previous Blue Note, Prestige, and EmArcy albums; the hissing noise is considerable, Rollins sounds unusually muffled, and, toward the end of the saxophone solo, what is apparently an inept edit destroys the musical continuity.

Sonny Rollins
The Sound of Sonny
Riverside RLP 12-241 (Original Jazz Classics OJC-029)
CD: Original Jazz Classics OJCCD029-2
Sonny Rollins (ts) Sonny Clark (p) Percy Heath (b), Roy Haynes (dr); New York, 6 /11–12/1957:
JUST IN TIME / MANGOES / CUTIE / IT COULD HAPPEN TO YOU / DEARLY BELOVED / EV'RY TIME WE SAY

GOODBYE / TOOT, TOOT, TOOTSIE
Same personnel, except Paul Chambers replaces Percy Heath; New York, 6/19/57:
WHAT IS THERE TO SAY / THE LAST TIME I SAW PARIS / FUNKY HOTEL BLUES

"Almost every album I've been on so far has been blowing eight choruses each on four or five tracks." Rollins' statement in the liner notes of his first album for Riverside as leader is perhaps a little exaggerated, but also prudent, as regards the danger of clichés in his recordings. This time Rollins wanted to do it differently. The original LP release contains nine tracks in 37 minutes ("Funky Hotel Blues," originally only on the Riverside sampler *Blues For Tomorrow*, was added to the *Sound Of Sonny* CD reissue). These are brief, well-ordered pieces which, unlike many Prestige LPs, show obvious care in their arrangement and rehearsal. Three recording dates had been made available, whereas with Bob Weinstock's low-budget label there would have been only one.

The tracks are also carefully chosen. They were meant to be standards (only "Cutie" is a Rollins original), but not warhorses. They include instead tunes most jazz musicians had left by the wayside. Among these were such pieces as the contemporary Rosemary Clooney hit "Mangoes" and the old Al Jolson number "Toot, Toot, Tootsie"–unexpected for jazz audiences and musicians, but representative of Rollins' trans-genre repertoire.

In Sonny Clark, Rollins found not only a namesake, but also a precise, trenchant pianist, whose spare, judicious comping leaves the saxophonist plenty of room. But Rollins seems to have tasted blood in the pianoless *Way Out West* recordings. On "The Last Time I Saw Paris," the piano has to sit out; and here, as on "Dearly Beloved," Rollins creates for himself even more free space with stop-time choruses. With "It Could Happen to You," he finally realizes what the lengthy *cadenzas* on previous records had only given a foretaste of: an unaccompanied saxophone solo. Alternating freely between a soaring rubato and precise, swinging runs, Rollins plays with the rudiments of the melody for a chorus and a half, finally abandoning it for a lengthy coda. This is a polished masterpiece, complete in itself, lasting a full four minutes and free of any virtuosic navel-gazing–a worthy successor to Coleman Hawkins' legendary unaccompanied solo on "Picasso."

Here, as on the remaining tracks, Rollins' playing seems more relaxed than on previous records: thoughtful, almost calm, conceived in large, sweeping arcs–certainly much less flamboyant than the improvisational flights on *Saxophone Colossus, Tour De Force* and *Way Out West.*

Abbey Lincoln
That's Him!

Riverside RLP 12-251 (Original Jazz Classics OJC-085)
CD: Original Jazz Classics OJCCD085-2
Abbey Lincoln (voc) Kenny Dorham (tp) Sonny Rollins (ts) Wynton Kelly (p, b on "Don't Explain") Paul Chambers (b) Max Roach (dr); New York, 10/28/57:
STRONG MAN / HAPPINESS IS JUST A THING CALLED JOE / MY MAN / TENDER AS A ROSE / THAT'S HIM / I MUST HAVE THAT MAN / PORGY / WHEN A WOMAN LOVES A MAN / DON'T EXPLAIN

Abbey Lincoln began her career as a nightclub singer, under pseudonyms such as "Anna Marie" and "Gaby Lee." For her first genuine jazz LP under her own name, Riverside producer Orrin Keepnews had created optimal conditions. The "Riverside Jazz All-Stars" credited on the cover were in actuality a first-rate quintet whose members were well suited to each other. Until a few months earlier, Rollins and Dorham had been part of Max Roach's quintet, and Chambers and Kelly were in on the project because they had been sidemen on previous Rollins LPs. But no one simply relied on the commercial potential of the big names; *That's Him!* is a record prepared with obvious care. This care is evident in the selection of some familiar and some rarely performed songs, all of which describe relationships from an imaginary female perspective (imaginary because the texts come from unmistakably male writers); it is also evident in the original, painstaking arrangements and their faultless execution.

This is not, as the liner notes claim, Rollins' "first recording with a singer"—there had already been the recordings with Babs Gonzales in 1949 and Earl Coleman in 1956—but it is, unfortunately, his last one to date. Here, as on the two vocal tracks of the *Tour De Force* LP, the saxophone player proves that he has mastered the refined art of sensitive accompaniment and annotation of a vocal line. And again, Rollins adopts the warm, muted tones of a Ben Webster or Lester Young for the occasion.

An instrumental curiosity as a side note: on "Don't Explain"—a track that, like several others, betrays Abbey Lincoln's admiration for Billie Holiday—the pianist Wynton Kelly substitutes for Paul Chambers on bass.

Sonny Rollins
A Night at the Village Vanguard
Blue Note BLP 1581 (BST 81581)
CD: Blue Note CDP 499 795-2
Sonny Rollins (ts) Wilbur Ware (b) Elvin Jones (dr); New York 11/3/57:
OLD DEVIL MOON / SOFTLY AS IN A MORNING SUNRISE / STRIVER'S ROW / SONNYMOON FOR TWO / I CAN'T GET STARTED

Sonny Rollins
More from the Vanguard
Blue Note BN-LA 475 H-2
CDs: Blue Note CDP 7 46517-2 / 7 46518-2
Sonny Rollins (ts) Donald Bailey (b) Pete LaRoca (dr); New York, 11/3/57:

He may not have invented the saxophone-bass-percussion trio, but Rollins set standards against which these formations are still measured today; and he did it especially with the Village Vanguard recordings. Rollins' first official live LP (at the same time, the first live recording made in Max Gordon's famous jazz club) delivers exactly what an earlier record title had promised: a tour de force. The two Blue Note releases contain over two hours of music, two hours of concentrated and exciting trio improvisations that require an almost superhuman effort–both of musical invention and physical exertion–on the saxophonist's part.

The repertoire is hardly noteworthy. Often-played standards predominate; even the two Rollins originals are only variations on familiar models. ("Striver's Row" is another themeless

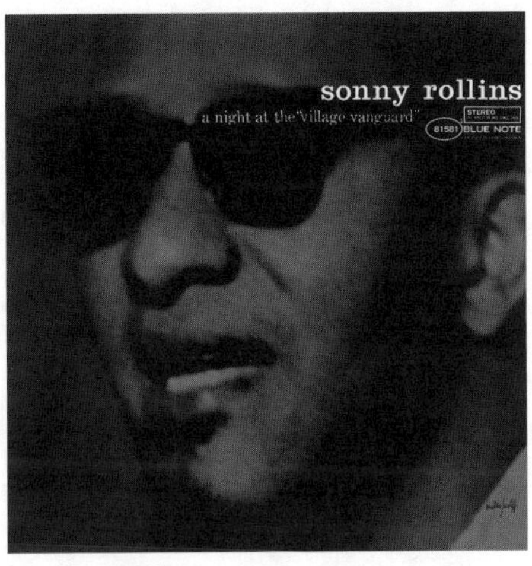

version of Parker's "Confirmation," and "Sonnymoon For Two" is a riff-based blues in B flat.) Nevertheless, the recordings are enlivened by a spirit of spontaneity, unpredictability, and experimentation. Unpredictability characterized Rollins' behavior even during preparations for the live recording. Although he had begun his guest spot at the Village Vanguard with a quintet, after a week he fired the trumpet player, a fate soon shared by the pianist. Not even the reduced trio survived intact; when the recording had already begun, Rollins decided he needed a new bassist and drummer. As a result, two tracks—probably recorded on the afternoon of November 3—feature Donald Bailey and Pete LaRoca, while the rest are performed with Wilbur Ware and Elvin Jones.

Equally unpredictable is what Rollins would do with the commonplace material. This becomes clear when comparing two versions of the same piece. The version of "Night in Tunisia" with Bailey and LaRoca is fast and hectic, and somewhat uneven in handling the polyrhythms of the A sections (a possible reason for Rollins' dissatisfaction with these sidemen). Later that same evening the piece is taken much more slowly, and capped by a long, dramatic saxophone cadenza. The two takes of Wilbur Ware's feature "Softly as in a Morning Sunrise" differ not just in tempo and solo allocation (the version on "More From The Vanguard" is slower and contains two bass solos), but also in Rollins' approach to the theme. In the *More from the Vanguard* version, he stretches the notes so slowly and thickly that it seems as if he were burlesquing the simple theme. He treats the other numbers in the same capricious manner. Almost nothing is faithful to the notes. The phrases are sometimes bent like an accordion, sometimes reduced to their basic intervals, then abbreviated to staccato shorthand–anything goes, so far as Rollins is concerned. The solos, too, exude this spirit of discovery, this joy in breaking down the compositions and playing with their elements. The "Sonnymoon For Two" riff describes a falling fifth–so Rollins isolates the fifth interval F–B flat and, for the length of three choruses, simply plays rhythmic variations with these two notes. Similarly, in "Woody'n You," single intervals or interval sequences are dissected and performed with variations. With these techniques, Rollins attains an improvisational rigor, a coherence of theme and solo, that one would seek in vain among his contemporaries. When the thematic ingredients have been exhausted, he simply quotes from other things–over the second-to-last chorus of "Woody'n You," for example, he drapes the beginning of the melody of "You Are Too Beautiful" at half its normal tempo.

In sum: this night at the Village Vanguard shows a Rollins who is in equal measure virtuosic, spontaneous, structurally conscientious, expressive, and humorous–in short, the classic Rollins before the bridge intermezzo. On top of that, it is a Rollins supported by Wilbur Ware and Elvin Jones–one of the finest rhythm sections of the time.

Note: on both CDs (*A Night at the Village Vanguard Vols. 1 and 2*), the material from the three LPs was rearranged–first come the tracks from the afternoon session with Bailey and LaRoca, then the tracks recorded later that evening with Ware and Jones.

Sonny Rollins
Sonny Rollins Plays
Period LP 1204
CD: Jazz Anthology 550 142
Sonny Rollins (ts) Jimmy Cleveland (tb) Gil Coggins (p) Wendell Marshall (b) Kenny Dennis (dr); New York, 11/4/57:
SONNYMOON FOR TWO / LIKE SOMEONE IN LOVE / THEME FROM PATHÉTIQUE SYMPHONY
(Three additional titles with different personnel, without Rollins)

These recordings have long been circulating in varying presentations and on different labels. Most of the time it is not clear from the cover that trumpet player Thad Jones plays on the B side in quintet and sextet recordings, and the title *First Recordings* under which these recordings occasionally appear (and which applies neither to Rollins nor to Jones) creates further confusion.

Such inconsistencies are no reason to ignore them, however. Because what Rollins offers here, only a day after the Village Vanguard marathon, is one of his most successful quintet recordings. The saxophone phrases, delivered with razor-sharp sound and precise intonation, connect beautifully with Jimmy Cleveland's velvety but virtuosic lines. Interesting repertoire and arrangements raise this production above the level of the innumerable typical hard-bop sessions. For the first time, Rollins is heard improvising on a theme from the world of "serious" music–and his heartfelt treatment of the melody from Tchaikovsky's "Symphonie Pathétique" defies the skeptics who see in it mere musical irony or jest. The carefully rehearsed saxophone counterpoint to the trombone melody, in the A sections of "Like Someone In Love," also bespeaks classical ambitions. These sections are distinguished from the B sections by the use of double time. And "Sonnymoon For Two" is, in this version, simply one of Rollins' most beautiful blues improvisations; he solos twice, once after the opening presentation of the theme in two brilliant stop-time choruses, and once with the rhythm section before the closing theme.

Dizzy Gillespie with Sonny Rollins and Sonny Stitt
Duets

Verve MGV 8260
CD: Verve J28J 25087
Dizzy Gillespie (tp) Sonny Rollins (ts) Ray Bryant (p) Tom Bryant (b) Charlie Persip (dr); New York, 12/11/57:
WHEATLEIGH HALL / SUMPHIN'
(Two or four (CD) additional titles with Stitt in place of Rollins)

Dizzy Gillespie / Sonny Stitt / Sonny Rollins
Sonny Side Up
Verve MGV 8262
CD: Verve 521 426-2
Dizzy Gillespie (tp, voc on "On the Sunny Side of the Street") Sonny Stitt, Sonny Rollins (ts) Ray Bryant (p) Tom Bryant (b) Charlie Persip (dr); New York, 12/19/57:
ON THE SUNNY SIDE OF THE STREET / THE ETERNAL TRIANGLE / AFTER HOURS / I KNOW THAT YOU KNOW

Anyone looking for representative recordings to demonstrate the strengths and weaknesses of hard bop in the late '50s could do worse than these two. Blinding virtuosity and sheer delight in playing go hand in hand with a reliance on cliché—cliché in regard both to the choice of repertoire (standards, "I Got Rhythm" variations, blues and more blues), and to the pattern-heavy improvisations.

Even if the nominal leader is Dizzy Gillespie, these are in effect two versions of the beloved "tenor battles" of the time. In *Duets* one can compare the playing styles of Stitt and Rollins on different pieces; on *Sonny Side Up* the two saxophone aces are heard simultaneously. Sonny Stitt, with his reputation as a Parker soundalike, was a fierce competitor in these cutting contests. His perfect control of the instrument, his effortless articulation, and his mastery at even the fastest tempos set an exacting standard–and Stitt was never one to hide his light under a bushel. But the Sonny Rollins of 1957 has no trouble matching him. His control of the tenor is no less than Stitt's; and like his colleague, six years his senior, Rollins has a rich arsenal of vocabulary in the Parker tradition to draw upon. But unlike Stitt, whose playing, with all its brilliance, can start to become a little repetitious after a while, Rollins is ever the rhythmically inventive soloist. The most exciting piece from the two sessions is unquestionably "The Eternal Triangle," Stitt's thoroughgoing paraphrase of "I Got Rhythm." Rollins' improvisation blends seamlessly into Stitt's solo, and in the ensuing exchange of four- and eight-bar phrases the two reach the heights of virtuosity and interaction found on Rollins' 1956 recording *Tenor Madness.* The only difference is that Rollins and Stitt are much closer stylistically than Coltrane and the Rollins of that time were. Their approach is so close that the dialogue at times becomes confusing. It must have been this similarity that caused Nat Hentoff, who wrote the liner notes for *Sonny Side Up*, to falsely assume that the first tenor solo on "On the Sunny Side of the Street" belonged to Stitt. In reality it is Rollins, who here–as elsewhere–can be indentifed by his darker sound and his hard, sometimes percussive, articulation. Otherwise, his harmonic and rhythmic playing is noticeably more conservative than on several previous recordings–maybe under pressure to meet the stylistic criteria of the bebop masters Stitt and Gillespie?

Sonny Rollins
Freedom Suite
Riverside RLP 12-258 (Original Jazz Classics OJC-067)
CD: Original Jazz Classics OJCCD 067-2
Sonny Rollins (ts) Oscar Pettiford (b) Max Roach (dr), New York, 2/27/58:
SOMEDAY I'LL FIND YOU / WILL YOU STILL BE MINE? / TILL THERE WAS YOU / SHADOW WALTZ
Same personnel and location, 3/7/58:
THE FREEDOM SUITE

Freedom Suite not only extends the series of great trio recordings that began with *Way Out West,* it also marks an advance in Rollins' ensemble play. For the first time, he succeeds in transcending the stereotyped theme-solo-theme format in favor of a larger and more complex structure, and also achieves a higher degree of teamwork among the three instruments than ever before. (This is described in greater detail in the chapter on Rollins the composer.)

The B side of the album, with four interpretations of Broadway tunes, is naturally less interesting, although there are plenty of worthy details. One of these is the one-bar (!) exchange between saxophone and percussion toward the end of "Someday I'll Find You." Another is the sensitive duet by Rollins and Pettiford on "Till There Was You," in which the

drums only feature as accompaniment for the bass solo. Here too, then, if only in small ways, are examples of Rollins' constant striving to enliven the conventional group dynamic with a structural and instrumental change of pace.

Apparently, it was only between the two recording dates that Rollins' scattered musical ideas coalesced in the innovative trio concept of the *Freedom Suite*. Riverside producer Orrin Keepnews recalls: "At the first session, we cut the four standards that appear on the other side of the record, and what I thought was a Rollins original. If he had any idea at that time of an entire suite, he was keeping it a secret from us. The second session was about a week later. There have been a lot of stories about trouble at the session, and there was some, but that's not important to the story. What is important is that the idea of a suite apparently grew in Sonny's mind in the time between the two sessions. I don't think he thought of it that way to begin with. When we went into the studio

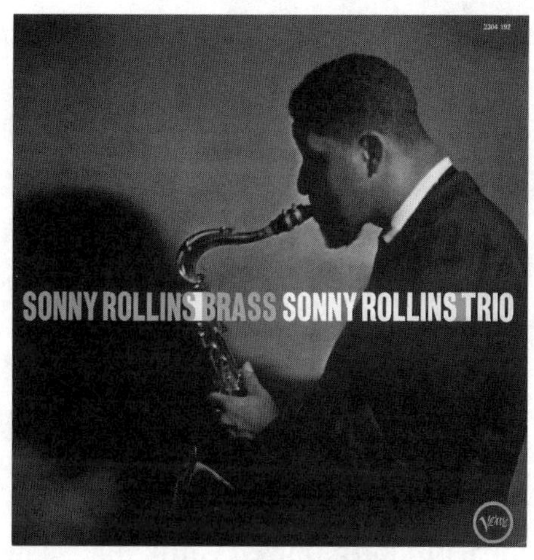

the second time, we cut the rest of it. It happened pretty spontaneously, that afternoon." (cited in Goldberg 1965a, 100) That the suite was pieced together after the fact from several segments recorded on different days is confirmed by the clearly audible breaks between segments.

Sonny Rollins/Brass
Sonny Rollins/Trio
Metrojazz 1002 (Verve MGV 8430)
CD: Verve 557545-2
Sonny Rollins (ts) Henry Grimes (b) Charles "Specs" Wright (dr); New York, 6/10/58:
WHAT'S MY NAME / IF YOU WERE THE ONLY GIRL IN THE WORLD / MANHATTAN / BODY AND SOUL (Rollins solo)
Sonny Rollins (ts) Nat Adderley (co) Clark Terry, Reunald Jones, Ernie Royal (tp) Billy Byers, Jimmy Cleveland, Frank Rehak (tb) Don Butterfield (tu) Dick Katz (p) René Thomas (g)

Henry Grlmes (b) Roy Haynes (dr) Ernie Wilkins (arr, cond); New York, 7/11/58:
WHO CARES? / LOVE IS A SIMPLE THING / GRAND STREET / FAR OUT EAST

The short-lived Metrojazz label was founded in 1958 as a subsidiary of the MGM Corporation. Producer Leonard Feather ensured a high artistic standard, and for the young label's second release something special had been planned. For the first time, Rollins–the undisputed tenor star–would be presented in an orchestral context, essentially a big band without woodwinds. This was probably not just the producer's idea, but harmonized with Rollins' own, inasmuch as he had, in interviews, continually expressed his interest in orchestral textures.

Unfortunately, the high expectations are not fulfilled. Ernie Wilkins' arrangements (he is known for his work with the Basie orchestra), though occasionally original–for example, a saxophone-tuba counterpoint in "Love is a Simple Thing"–are altogether not much more than a massive framing of and (occasional) background music for Rollins' solo excursions. There is no true integration of the soloist, or marriage of improvisation and orchestral phrases. The level of interplay found in the contemporary recordings of Miles Davis and Gil Evans remains out of reach.

The B side shows a newly staffed Rollins trio that has a hard time living up to the standards established on *Way Out West* and *Freedom Suite.* The most rewarding thing on this record is Rollins' unaccompanied solo on "Body and Soul"–a candid tribute to the art of his role model Coleman Hawkins.

Newport Jazz 1958–59
FDC 1024
Sonny Rollins (ts) Henry Grimes (b) Roy Haynes (dr); Newport, 7/7/58:
I WANT TO BE HAPPY
(Additional tracks with different musicians, without Rollins)

The one track on this sampler of various recordings from the Newport Jazz Festival is hardly an indispensable addition to Rollins' already well-documented trio work. True, this formation, with Roy Haynes on drums, is rarely documented on record; but the drums are hard to hear on the technically uneven tape. The music, on the other hand, is first-rate: the 1924 Vincent Youmans hit, performed at a frantic clip, once again inspires Rollins to intricate explorations of interval and rhythm.

Sonny Rollins at Music Inn
Terry Edwards at Falcon's Lair with Joe Castro
Metrojazz 1011
Sonny Rollins (ts) John Lewis (p on "John's Other Theme" and "You Are Too Beautiful") Percy Heath (b) Connie Kay (dr); Lenox, Mass., 8/3/58:
JOHN'S OTHER THEME / LIMEHOUSE BLUES/ I'LL FOLLOW MY SECRET HEART / YOU ARE TOO BEAUTIFUL
(Two additional tracks with the Teddy Edwards quartet, without Rollins)

The Modern Jazz Quartet at Music Inn
Guest Artist: Sonny Rollins
Atlantic 1299
CD: Atlantic 7567-80794-2

Sonny Rollins (ts) Milt Jackson (vib) John Lewis (p) Percy Heath (b) Connie Kay (dr); Lenox, Mass., 8/3/58:
BAGS' GROOVE / NIGHT IN TUNISIA
(Four additional tracks without Rollins)

At the Music Inn, only a few minutes from Tanglewood, three-week-long summer courses were held under John Lewis' direction beginning in 1957. One of the attractions of the second session of the "School of Jazz" was the first meeting between Sonny Rollins and the Modern Jazz Quartet since the 1953 Prestige recordings (*Sonny Rollins with the Modern Jazz Quartet*). Only two tracks represent a complete reunion; the other two are interpreted in a trio or quartet format. The unfortunate division of the concert recording–which resulted in two heterogeneous LPs–probably goes back to horse trading between Metrojazz producer Leonard Feather and his Atlantic colleague Nesuhi Ertegun. Both of the tracks with the complete Modern Jazz Quartet were allotted to MJQ's host label Atlantic, while the four remaining went to Rollins' label Metrojazz. This is unfortunate, because it was just this contrast between the different combinations of musicians that was the main attraction of the concert (outstandingly captured by Atlantic engineer Tom Dowd).

The trio with Heath and Kay, for instance, demonstrates completely different qualities from the others Rollins played in at the time–the ones with Ray Brown/Shelly Manne, Wilbur Ware/Elvin Jones, and Oscar Pettiford/Max Roach. The solos of the sidemen on *Way Out West* and *Freedom Suite* are undeniably more distinctive, and the Ware/Jones team is more forceful. But the sonorous steadiness of Percy Heath, coupled with the crystalline cymbal work of Connie Kay, complements Rollins' improvisations beautifully. Rollins himself is in fine form this evening, and dispels memories of routine playing on previous records. At the same time, these recordings make it abundantly clear why his playing was consistently described as "ironic" or "sardonic." The droll way he has of willfully slurring, distorting, and fragmenting the melodies is notable, not only on the modern jazz standards, but even on "Limehouse Blues," from 1922. But this art of derangement is more than whimsy. The range of articulation, the subtle gradations of tone, the tension-filled stretching and contracting of the phrases, the dynamic sweep, the alternation of notes and rests, the way he sometimes sticks closely to, sometimes distances himself from the themes–all these are musical qualities *per se*, that once again establish Sonny Rollins as the most accomplished saxophonist of his time.

A note: the Rollins classic "Doxy" can be heard lurking behind "John's Other Theme."

Sonny Rollins
Newk's Time
Blue Note 4001
CD: Blue Note CDP 784001-2
Sonny Rollins (ts) Wynton Kelly (p) Doug Watkins (b) Philly Joe Jones (dr); Hackensack, 8/28/58:
TUNE UP / ASIATIC RAES / WONDERFUL! WONDERFUL! / THE SURREY WITH THE FRINGE ON TOP / BLUES FOR PHILLY JOE / NAMELY YOU

Rollins had avoided the classic bebop-quartet format on

records since *The Sound Of Sonny*. *Newk's Time*, however, Rollins' last Blue Note LP, is less a return to, than (as Jack Cooke put it) "a formal farewell to the New York hard-bop school within which he emerged and which he was now rapidly outgrowing." (Cooke 1986, 64) Not until 1962 would Rollins reenter a recording studio on the East Coast (*The Bridge*). So *Newk's Time* affirms Rollins' mastery in the standard quartet setting and takes stock of his accomplishments without, however, offering anything new or unexpected. Not that this production is a waste; many details are worth hearing. For example: the clever meter and tempo changes on Kenny Dorham's "Asiatic Raes" and the saxophone–drum duo on "The Surrey With The Fringe On Top"–to my knowledge a discographic first, years before melody–rhythm duos were popularized by John Coltrane. And the "Blues for Billy Joe"–the only Rollins original on the record–is an especially compelling example of a saxophone improvisation rigorous in its use of thematic motifs; it thus deserves a place alongside the celebrated "Blue Seven" from *Saxophone Colossus.*

Sonny Rollins and The Contemporary Leaders: Barney Kessel, Hampton Hawes, Leroy Vinnegar, Shelly Manne

Contemporary M 3564/S 7564 (Original Jazz Classics OJC-340)
CD: Original Jazz Classics OJCCD 340-2

Sonny Rollins (ts) Barney Kessel (g) Hampton Hawes (p) Leroy Vinnegar (b) Shelly Manne (dr) Victor Feldman (vib on "You"); Los Angeles, 10/20–22/58:

I'VE TOLD EVERY LITTLE STAR / ROCKA-BYE YOUR BABY WITH A DIXIE MELODY / HOW HIGH THE MOON / YOU / I'VE FOUND A NEW BABY / ALONE TOGETHER / IN THE CHAPEL IN THE MOONLIGHT / THE SONG IS YOU

The lineup of Rollins' last studio LP before the legendary Bridge hiatus seems, at first glance, to run contrary to his preferences at the time. Where he had freed himself from the bonds of piano accompaniment in the trio performances, here he is dealing with two harmony instruments. But the concerns are unfounded. Barney Kessel and Hampton Hawes are so sparing, precise, and responsive, that nowhere is there a sense of restriction–only of a more colorful, variegated group sound. Still, the most beautiful piece on the record is one with a reduced lineup. A spontaneous jam on "How High the Moon"–Mann and Hawes had not yet arrived at the studio–unites Rollins, Kessel and Vinnegar in the relaxed, equally balanced chamber jazz that was a trademark of West Coast jazz in these years. For once the maestro Rollins does not lord it over his

sidemen, but submits to the artistry of give-and-take, of economy, of brief formulations, that is essential to the success of this sort of intimate trio work. The dialogue with Barney Kessel is especially rewarding. In the closing presentation of the theme, Rollins shows how one can turn an error—a tripped-over note—to account, making it the subject of an improvisation. The art of reduction comes into play on "I've Found a New Baby," where Rollins juggles the timbral and rhythmic elements of a single pitch over the course of several choruses. Especially notable is the selection of *retro* numbers on the record—as if he wanted to substantiate the statement made in the liner notes: "I have a lot of respect for the art [of jazz], you know, and for the tradition. Jazz is a thing that is only built upon what has happened before. It doesn't begin with any one guy. The greatest anybody can be is just as great as what has come before, and to be great you have to be steeped in what has happened." Only once does Rollins disturb the beautiful mood of cooperation among the five equal partners: in the headlong tempo of "The Song is You," the four West Coast musicians are reduced to breathless bit players chasing after the saxophone, and even the fine Vinnegar–Manne rhythm team loses its momentum.

Sonny Rollins
Contemporary Alternate Takes
Contemporary C-7651
Sonny Rollins (ts) Ray Brown (b) Shelly Manne (dr); Los Angeles, 3/7/57:
I'M AN OLD COWHAND / COME, GONE WAY OUT WEST
Sonny Rollins (ts) Barney Kessel (g) Hampton Hawes (p) Leroy Vinnegar (b) Shelly Manne (dr) Victor Feldman (vib on "You"); Los Angeles, 10/22/58:
THE SONG IS YOU / YOU / I'VE FOUND A NEW BABY

It was not until 1985 that these treasures from Contemporary producer Lester Koenig's archive were made available to the public, leftovers from the two sessions that Rollins had recorded for the West Coast label. There is no new material here, just alternate takes of preexisting tracks. The fact that these were passed over at the time could only have been because of little things that irritated Rollins, a notorious perfectionist: here and there the squeak of a reed or a tripped-over saxophone note, a somewhat rocky finish ("Way Out West"), a flubbed start (Rollins' premature entrance on the closing theme of "I'm an Old Cowhand") or something as trivial as the sound of a bottle tipping over (during the bass solo of "Come, Gone"). As regards inspiration and soloistic creativity, the alternate takes are certainly no worse than the master takes, in some places even better. The fact that Rollins' venturous solo on "I've Found A New Baby," experimenting with articulation and boldly venturing into the alto register, can now be heard on record, is a real plus. In general, however, the differences in tempo, construction and musical quality are so subtle that the alternate takes represent a nice addition, but no significant departure.

Sonny Rollins Trio
In Stockholm 1959
St. Thomas
Dragon DRLP 73
CD: Dragon DRCD 229
Sonny Rollins (ts) Henry Grimes (b) Pete LaRoca (dr);
Stockholm, 3/1–3/1959:
ST. THOMAS
Same personnel, Stockholm, 3/4/59:

THERE WILL NEVER BE ANOTHER YOU / STAY AS SWEET AS YOU ARE / I'VE TOLD EVERY LITTLE STAR / HOW HIGH THE MOON / OLEO / PAUL'S PAL

Sonny Rollins Trio
In Sweden 1959
Ingo 9
Sonny Rollins (ts) Henry Grimes (b) Pete LaRoca (dr); Stockholm, 3/4/59:
THERE WILL NEVER BE ANOTHER YOU / I'VE TOLD EVERY LITTLE STAR / STAY AS SWEET AS YOU ARE / OLEO / PAUL'S PAL / IT DON'T MEAN A THING / PAUL'S PAL / LOVE LETTERS

Sonny Rollins
Sonnymoon For Two
Moon Records MC D 0 1 5-2
Sonny Rollins (ts) Henry Grimes (b) Pete LaRoca; Zurich, 3/5/59:
I REMEMBER YOU / I'VE TOLD EVERY LITTLE STAR / OLEO / WILL YOU STILL BE MINE / IT COULD HAPPEN TO YOU
Sonny Rollins (ts) Kenny Drew (p) Niels-Henning Orsted-Pedersen (b) Albert Heath (dr); Copenhagen, 9/6/68:
SONNYMOON FOR TWO

Sonny Rollins
Aix-en-Provence, 1959
Royal Jazz RJ 502
Sonny Rollins (ts) Henry Grimes (b) Kenny Clarke (dr); Aix-en-Provence, 3/11/59:
WOODY'N YOU / BUT NOT FOR ME / LADY BIRD

Although the first edition of Thorbjørn Sjøgren's commendable discography, published in 1983, indicates a gap between the *Contemporary Leaders* LP from October 1958 and *The Bridge* from January/February 1962, in the past few years a whole slew of recordings from Rollins' first European tour in February/March 1959 have come onto the market, providing us with a more accurate picture of Rollins' playing just before his two-year sabbatical. Stylistically, as is to be expected, they recall the Village Vanguard concert of November 1957–it is the high art of playing standards, reduced to the essentials of melody, harmony and rhythm, with all the freedom made possible by the reduced trio lineup.

The repertoire of the Swedish LP is retrospective: the three Rollins compositions first appeared on record in 1954 ("Oleo") and 1956 ("St. Thomas," "Paul's Pal"). Rollins even begins his solo on "St. Thomas" with the same rhythmically displaced phrase that introduced his solo on *Saxophone Colossus.* Still, the version recorded in the Stockholm jazz club "Nalen" is more impressive–so impressive, in fact, that the Rollins fan who recorded it was inspired to press it onto a 45 edition of a mere ten (!) copies–a discographical treasure that was made available to a wider listening audience only in 1984 with the Dragon release. The rest of the tracks of the *St. Thomas* LP come from a studio production by the Swedish National Radio. Rollins greets listeners with, "Good afternoon, jazz fans; this is Sonny Rollins in Sweden," and the rest of his announcements are also preserved.

While Rollins pushes the theme's phrases chromatically back and forth in "There Will Never Be Another You," he applies this technique of tension-filled displacement to the note lengths on the theme of "How High the Moon." Pete LaRoca and Henry Grimes prove themselves not only a well integrated, impressive rhythm section, but on "How High the Moon"–a practice take that was not intended for broadcast–they are especially impressive in bass-drum fours that show off their solo abilities.

The material that the Swedish radio finally released from its archives, after 25 years, had already been published on the notorious Italian pirate label Ingo. The first five tracks of the Ingo LP–whose lineup and track titles are wrong, but have been corrected above–are nothing more than the corresponding tracks of the Dragon record, but without announcements, partly incomplete, and technically less satisfactory. Obviously, a Swedish amateur sent his broadcast recording to Italy. Even the three additional pieces, which, judging from the static, were also recorded off the radio, offer no musical revelations to commend this bootleg LP.

Even though the Rollins trio was in the same top form the next day in Zurich, the *Sonnymoon For Two* release is just as hard to recommend as the Ingo LP. For one thing, the sound quality–here, again, evidently a radio recording–is noticeably worse than the Dragon production; for another, this recording is clearly an illegal bootleg. Only the unaccompanied first chorus of "It Could Happen To You" (as compared to the solo version on "The Sound Of Sonny") adds something new to the playing on the Dragon LP. The 1968 recording, intended to round out the twenty-five minutes of music from 1959, might seem a compelling reason to buy, since Rollins recordings between the "official" LPs of 1966 (*East Broadway Run Down*) and 1972 (*Next Album*) are rare. In the event, the 20-minute "Sonnymoon For Two" performance at the Montmartre in Copenhagen is disappointing. The sound quality is miserable, and Rollins' improvisation, though played with verve, is fairly conventional both melodically and harmonically, caught up in blues and pentatonic formulas. Since Kenny Drew's piano solo is almost inaudible, the actual highlight turns out to be the bravura bass solo by local hot shot Niels-Henning Orsted-Pedersen.

The recording from the south of France, released in 1989, is a real sensation, however. Is it merely the replacement of Pete LaRoca with Kenny Clarke, the bop percussion pioneer, that inspires Rollins to such heights? In three tracks of over a quarter of an hour each, he draws on all his improvisational skills, making the previous recordings from only a few days earlier seem downright tame and clichéd. The widely held opinion that the "conservative" Rollins only attained to a modern style in 1962, under the influence of Coleman sidemen Don Cherry and Billy Higgins, is belied by these three tracks. Rollins preserves the form of the compositions (unlike the 1962 recordings), but within this framework radically deconstructs the motivic, harmonic and rhythmic structures from the ground up. The theme of the Dizzy Gillespie classic "Woody'n You" is at first completely unrecognizable, and only emerges bar by bar from the fragmentary phrases. And by stretching the melodic material to the extremes of the low and high registers (never before has Rollins ventured so far into high harmonics), similarly straining the harmonic structure, and dissolving the bebop phrases into indistinct ribbons of notes, Rollins tightens the musical bow to its limit, only to relax it again in melodically catchy, harmonically simple, and rhythmically straightforward passages. (He does not skimp on quotations in the process, from Bach and Prokofiev to "St. Thomas" and "Alexander's Ragtime Band.")

These alternations between convention and defiance of convention are precisely what give the three pieces their excitement. Harry Grimes' bass unfortunately remains in the background throughout, a fault of the recording equipment. Not to be missed, however, is the practically telepathic exchange of synchronous accents between Rollins and Clarke on "Lady Bird." "Yeah, that was a ball," the chronically dissatisfied saxophone player is heard to say at the end of the set. And after this tour de force, it is hard to hold against him his refusal to do an encore, pleading, "Je suis fatigué!"

Sonny Rollins
The Bridge
RCA LPM/LSP-2527
CD: RCA 2119278-2
Sonny Rollins (ts) Jim Hall (g) Bob Cranshaw (b) Harry T. Saunders (dr); New York. 1/30/62:
GOD BLESS THE CHILD
Same personnel, but Ben Riley replaces Saunders; New York, 2/13/62:
JOHN S. / YOU DO SOMETHING TO ME / WHERE ARE YOU
Same personnel; New York, 2/14/62:
WITHOUT A SONG / THE BRIDGE

Expectations for Sonny Rollins' comeback record were huge–so huge that it was perhaps inevitable that *The Bridge* met with politely veiled disappointment in the media. Because, despite what had been expected, hoped, or feared, *The Bridge* does not evince any radical change in style, and does not present any markedly new approach. So–business as usual? That conclusion would fail to do justice to the value of this record, because under the unspectacular surface lurk several innovative particulars.

The opening of the album, "Without A Song," is seemingly staid. But even here, if one listens closely, there are details–sudden switches from metrical playing to a free rubato and back, carefully conceived accompanying figures behind the bass solo for saxophone and guitar–that suggest not only intense preparation, but also an ongoing effort to deepen and diversify the interaction between the instruments in the jazz

ensemble. Most of these fine points in the combo playing, however, are "not set routines," as Rollins stresses in the album notes, "but are felt by the group"–i.e., the result of spontaneous interplay. This atmosphere of a mature, communicative, sometimes chamber music-like cohesion runs through the music of *The Bridge* like a red thread. The participation of Jim Hall, whose playing is both responsive and structurally grounded, has a catalyzing effect.

The masterpiece among these interpretations of standards is "God Bless the Child." This piece contains tricky but quite natural shifts between meter and rubato, free handling of the parts of the form, and harmonic sophistication in the way Rollins, Hall, and Cranshaw refine and stretch the chord progressions of Billie Holiday's melody. The time-honored rhythm changes, for decades a favorite of jazz soloists, is also treated to a new variation. The motif making up the theme of "The

Bridge" is simple, containing only the notes B, C and D, but what is unusual is the four-bar alternation of 4/4 and 3/4 time (in the tempo relation 4:3), which Rollins uses to loosen up the A sections of the 32-bar AABA form.

These innovations are not only to be found in the more familiar pieces. With "John S.," Rollins presents a quite unconventionally structured piece. A three-part structure in fragmented 3/4 time frames improvisations on a 34-bar (18+16) chorus. This is preceded by a 32-bar theme melodically reduced to a descending minor triad.

As for Rollins the saxophonist, he remains recognizably the same. His sound is softer, less contoured. In "The Bridge" and "John S." the harmonic liberties and chromatic departures first heard on the March 1959 recording in Aix-en-Provence are heard once more.

Sonny Rollins
What's New?
RCA LPM/LSP-2572
CD: RCA 2119311-2
Sonny Rollins (ts) Jim Hall (g) Bob Cranshaw (b) Ben Riley (dr); New York 4/5/62:
THE NIGHT HAS A THOUSAND EYES
Same personnel, plus Willie Rodriguez, Dennis Charles, Frank Charles (perc) and choir (arr and cond: Jimmy Jones); New York, 4/25/62:
DON'T STOP THE CARNIVAL
Same personnel; New York, 4/26/62:
BROWNSKIN GIRL
Sonny Rollins (ts) Bob Cranshaw (b) Candido Camero (perc);

New York, 5/14/62:
JUNGOSO / BLUESONGO

It was guitarists who first infected the U.S. jazz scene with the bossa nova bug. Charlie Byrd had traveled Latin America in 1961 and become acquainted with the brand-new music of Joao Gilberto and Antonio Carlos Jobim, and in 1960 Jim Hall had made cross-cultural musical connections on a tour of South America with Ella Fitzgerald.

The marketing experts at RCA were right to sense great commercial promise in the combination of bossa nova and jazz. The *Jazz Samba* LP by Charlie Byrd and Stan Getz, recorded only two months before *What's New?*, was a bestseller. It is therefore understandable that the cover of Rollins' second RCA LP abounds with references to the new "rhythm from Brazil." This is misleading, however. Strictly speaking, only the quartet's polished interpretation of the film-noir tune "The

Night Has a Thousand Eyes" has anything in common with bossa nova. Rollins' unique take on the marriage of Latin American and Afro-American music relates to his Caribbean roots rather than the bossa trend. Calypso had been a trademark of Rollins' work since "St. Thomas" (1956), and the pieces "Don't Stop the Carnival" and "Brownskin Girl" are authentic calypso melodies. Here, they are offered up with inspired improvisations, but unfortunately also with a choral accompaniment that exudes a beer-hall conviviality (courtesy of arranger Jimmy Jones).

Other jazz-Latin encounters, more difficult to classify, are found on the two trio tracks. "Bluesongo," as the name suggests, is a simple blues with conga accompaniment, while "Jungoso" is the most experimental and exciting piece on the record. Over a two-bar bass ostinato Rollins and the conga player Candido conduct a breathtaking conversation in which Rollins' playing is rhythmic and melodically simple, but unorthodox in tone. The saxophone harshens to a growl, expands to multiphonics, distorted by over-blowing techniques. At times the bass pauses and leaves the field to the two interlocutors, resulting in dense interactions between these two representatives of melody and rhythm. Note: "Don't Stop The Carnival" was not included on the initial American release of *What's New?*

Sonny Rollins
Our Man in Jazz
RCA LPM/LSP 2612
CD: RCA 211 9256-2
Sonny Rollins (ts) Don Cherry (co) Bob Cranshaw (b) Billy

Higgins (dr); New York, 7/29–30/62:
OLEO / DEARLY BELOVED / DOXY

Ornette Coleman and his associates had already gotten to know and appreciate Rollins' playing in the late '50s on his brief visits to the West Coast. After Don Cherry and Billy Higgins, who had moved to New York with Coleman at the end of 1959, left the free-jazz pioneer's quartet, Rollins–always on the lookout for new musical encounters–took the opportunity to team up. Even though Cherry and Higgins unmistakably bring along their experience with Coleman's music, the musical framework of these three tracks (recorded live at the Village Gate in New York) is still dictated by Rollins. For one thing, the compositions are either Rollins' own or come from his repertoire. For another, the playing on display here corresponds more to Rollins' than to Coleman's idea of musical freedom (as Ekkehard Jost convincingly argues in the Don Cherry chapter of his book *Free Jazz* (Jost 1975, p. 160f.). While Coleman, for all his liberties with harmony and meter, tends to stick closely to the traditional structure of a piece, Rollins, while he may be more conventional in terms of melody and harmony, is more open in terms of form.

This can be seen in the case of "Oleo." Rollins' classic theme may be the starting point and common frame of reference for the 25-minute improvisation, but the musical whole develops in a spontaneous process of collective improvisation. In theory, this musical whole could be described as a (fairly standard) sequence of saxophone, bass and trumpet solos, but the spontaneous reactions of the musicians constantly create new instrumental combinations and textures that break

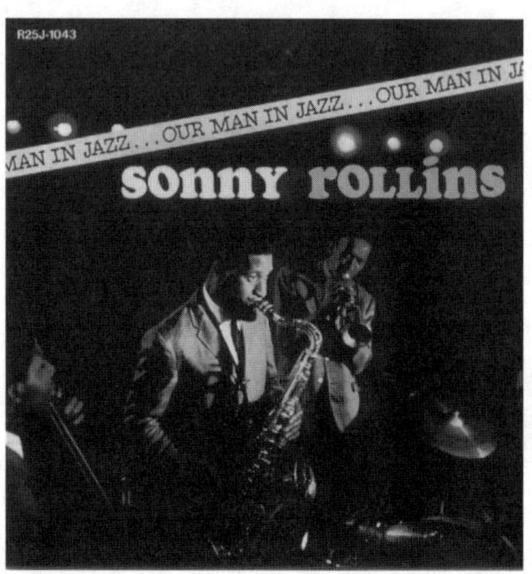

through this routine. (In fact, it is precisely this dialectic between convention and defiance of convention that creates the tension in Rollins' music from this period.) For example, the two horns' commentaries turn a bass solo by Bob Cranshaw into a chamber-music-like trio. Rollins is also clearly interested in picking up on and elaborating ideas from the other musicians. In this spirit he undertakes to emulate the high trumpet phrases and drum figures, using a range expanded into the altissimo register and imitating trumpet sounds and percussion. (The fact that, aside from the intuition and spontaneity, some things had been arranged beforehand is indicated by the unison horn riff that frames Billy Higgins' solo.)

If communication is Rollins' strong point in this music, his solo passages leave a conflicting impression. The liberation of harmony and broadening of the sound spectrum open up improvisational possibilities that Rollins takes full advantage of;

at the same time, his exploration of these possibilities sometimes seems tentative, aimless, even formulaic. One can sense his uncertainty, confronted with so many choices, about his stylistic identity. Is this what prompts him, after a good 18 minutes, when nothing is left of the form and chord progression of "Oleo," to insist on suddenly intoning a blues that seems to ignore what his fellow musicians are doing? He continues to tread familiar territory until the other three fall in line.

While "Oleo" impresses one as a voyage of musical discovery, Rollins' treatment of the standard "Dearly Beloved" is certainly a caricature. Tempo changes, phrase deformations, waltz and march rhythms transform the genial Jerome Kern number into a musical grotesquerie. Rollins' sarcasm is, however, also ready to turn on itself, as evidenced by his markedly odd counterpoint to the cornet melody on "Doxy," otherwise the most conventional piece on this album. Here, form, meter, and harmony are all assailed in the solos–and Rollins rattles the bars of the cage of convention much more vigorously than Cherry.

3 In Jazz
Gary Burton–Sonny Rollins–Clark Terry
RCA LPM/LSP-2725
Sonny Rollins (ts) Don Cherry (co) Henry Grimes (b) Billy Higgins (dr); New York, 2/20/63:
I COULD WRITE A BOOK / YOU ARE MY LUCKY STAR / THERE WILL NEVER BE ANOTHER YOU
(Eight additional tracks [four each of the Gary Burton Quartet and the Clark Terry Quintet])

The last recordings of the Rollins–Cherry quartet–and the group's one and only studio production–is found on a fairly obscure RCA sampler that, to my knowledge, was never re-released. The three Rollins tracks, however, were added to the French RCA's double-LP reissue of *What's New? / Our Man in Jazz.*

The finale of this innovative collaboration is surprisingly conservative. Three familiar standards, all of them structured with 32 beats in the ABA'B pattern and played at medium tempo, are performed with the usual sequence of (brief) solos. The strength of this outfit–the free interaction, the spontaneous breaking down of traditional contexts–is really only heard on the coda to "There Will Never Be Another You."

Sonny Rollins and Coleman Hawkins
Sonny Meets Hawk!
RCA LPM/LSP-2712
CD: RCA 2122107-2
Sonny Rollins, Coleman Hawkins (ts) Paul Bley (p) Bob Cranshaw (b) Roy McCurdy (dr); New York, 7/15/63:
ALL THE THINGS YOU ARE / LOVER MAN / YESTERDAYS
Same personnel, but Henry Grimes replaces Bob Cranshaw; New York, 7/18/63:
JUST FRIENDS / AT McKIE'S / SUMMERTIME

Staged encounters between jazz greats are usually a bit stiff. Often they are the idea of producers with their mind on the money more than the music. And the results are often polite musical gestures, non-committal phrases, a tentative playing toward or even around one another.

Any such misgivings are quickly dispelled by this album, which followed a joint live appearance by the two at the Newport Jazz Festival. For Rollins, this encounter with his childhood idol must have fulfilled a real artistic ambition. More importantly, however, Rollins is not the sort of musician to deny his musical temperament just to find a modicum of common ground. Quite the opposite–here it is the avant-garde Rollins who shows up alongside the "father of jazz saxophone" (as Hawkins is called on the cover). Rollins' reading of the overworked standards combines keen reinterpretation with unorthodox technique.

Despite all this, one senses a lot of love and respect in this meeting of two generations. Rollins carefully avoids pushing the aging "Hawk" to the wall with his virtuosity. He gives him room, picks up on his ideas and refines them (for example, on "Yesterdays," where Rollins constructs an entire chorus of trills from the closing trill in Hawkins' solo). Hawkins, for his part, is clearly inspired by the unfamiliar company (even Paul Bley plays just about everything but the "official" harmonies). Nicest are the numerous choruses in which the two tenors play together not as a tenor battle, but in a kind of civilized father–son dialogue. One gets an idea of what tradition and advancing the tradition can mean in jazz, what the connections are, where they divide.

The most unusual product of the two studio dates is perhaps Rollins' piece "At McKies." It is less a "theme" in the traditional sense than a four-bar phrase, used as the starting point for a free improvisation around the key of B flat. Hawkins demonstrates that he can make something of this exotic material even without the harmonic support of the piano, which sits out for long stretches.

Sonny Rollins
Now's The Time!
RCA LPM/LSP-2927
CD: RCA R25J-1011
Sonny Rollins (ts) Thad Jones (co) Bob Cranshaw (b) Roy McCurdy (dr); New York, 1/20/64:
52ND STREET THEME
Sonny Rollins (ts) Ron Carter (b) Roy McCurdy (dr); New York, 2/14/64:
ST. THOMAS
Same personnel plus Herbie Hancock (p); same date and location:
NOW'S THE TIME / 'ROUND MIDNIGHT
Same personnel, same location, 2/18/64:

AFTERNOON IN PARIS
Sonny Rollins (ts) Bob Cranshaw (b) Roy McCurdy (dr); New York, 4/14/64:
BLUE 'N' BOOGIE / I REMEMBER CLIFFORD / FOUR

Sonny Rollins & Co.
The Standard Sonny Rollins
RCA LPM/LSP-3355
CD: RCA 2122109-2
Sonny Rollins (ts) Jim Hall (g) Herbie Hancock (p) Teddy Smith, David Izenzon (b) Stu Martin (dr); New York, 6/11/64:
TRAV'LIN' LIGHT
Sonny Rollins (ts) Bob Cranshaw (b) Mickey Roker (dr); New York, 6/23/64:
I'LL BE SEEING YOU
Same personnel, same location, 6/24/64:
THREE LITTLE WORDS / NIGHT AND DAY
Same personnel plus Jim Hall (g); same date and location:

MY SHIP

Same personnel, same location, 6/26/64:

LOVE LETTERS / LONG AGO (AND FAR AWAY)

Sonny Rollins (ts) Herbie Hancock (p) Bob Cranshaw (b) Mickey Roker (dr); New York, 7/2/64:

IT COULD HAPPEN TO YOU / MY ONE AND ONLY LOVE

Same personnel but without Herbie Hancock; New York,7/9/64:

AUTUMN NOCTURNE

Sonny Rollins

The Alternative Rollins

RCA PL 43268

Sonny Rollins (ts) Thad Jones (co) Bob Cranshaw (b) Roy McCurdy (dr); New York, 1/20/64:

I REMEMBER CLIFFORD

Sonny Rollins (ts) Ron Carter (b) Roy McCurdy (dr); New York, 1/24/64:

ST. THOMAS / 52ND STREET THEME / FOUR

Same personnel plus Herbie Hancock (p); same date and location:

DJANGO / AFTERNOON IN PARIS / NOW'S THE TIME / FOUR

Sonny Rollins (ts) Jim Hall (g) Herbie Hancock (p) Teddy Smith, David Izenzon (b) Stu Martin (dr); New York, 6/11/64:

TRAV'LIN' LIGHT

Sonny Rollins (ts) Herbie Hancock (p) Bob Cranshaw (b) Mickey Roker (dr); New York, 7/2/64:

WINTER IN WONDERLAND / WHEN YOU WISH UPON A STAR

What a difference from the Prestige years. While at Prestige an afternoon generally sufficed to record an entire LP, the production of Rollins' last two RCA albums was a very protracted affair. Between January and July of 1964, according to Thorbjørn Sjøgren's discography, Sonny Rollins went into RCA's Studio B no fewer than thirteen times, and in addition to various other sidemen, four drummers and four bassists got involved. While the results of the first two recording dates–involving Elvin Jones, among others–have still not been released, sessions 3, 5, 6 and 7 became the album *Now's The Time!* Sessions 8 and 13 became *The Standard Sonny Rollins.*

Key word: "standard." The interpretation of standards was basic to all these recordings. Why the great expense, why so much time and effort for something apparently so mundane? Because Rollins intends to make the ordinary extraordinary. As practiced here, the playing of standards has nothing to do with habit. On the contrary: the well-known pieces are a pretext for great experimentation. Hence the wide array of lineups, from various trios to the unusual sextet combination of sax, guitar, piano, two basses (one plucked, one bowed), and drums ("Trav'lin' Light"). The musical approaches range equally wide, from relatively orthodox interpretations, to improvisational dismantling of harmony and meter. And the sound of the saxophone varies greatly even between chronologically close takes (compare, for example, "Night And Day" from the 24th of June with "Love Letters" two days later).

The shortest and, comparatively speaking, most straightforward versions are the ones that can be heard on *Now's The Time!* and *The Standard Sonny Rollins.* The tracks on the first

LP seem relatively complete, but the second one occasionally gives the impression that the piece has ended before the improvisational ideas have really developed. In addition, the editorial interventions on this record are drastic. Even more irritating than the repeated fadeouts are the clumsy tape edits that abruptly terminate the piano solo on "It Could Happen to You" and make the end of "Long Ago (And Far Away)" seem so clumsy. (In this respect, it is somewhat puzzling that Rollins, the perfectionist, has said of this record in particular: "The only one of my records that I'm completely satisfied with is the album with standards that I made for RCA. Yeah, that's the record I consider my best." (Postif 1989, 83)).

In light of these deficiencies, the double LP *The Alternative Rollins*—released years later—proves a belated corrective. Eleven tracks from sessions 3, 4, 8 and 12 can be heard here—seven of them from the unusually productive January 24 session that is elsewhere undocumented—and there are not just alternate takes, but include some new songs as well. There is hardly any disruptive technical interference, and what was barely suggested on the preceding records is made explicit here—particularly on "Now's The Time" and "52nd Street Theme." In these two quarter-of-an-hour solo flights, Rollins gives an account of practically everything he knew in 1964 about the basic forms of the blues and of rhythm changes. This can be seen in the way he strains the harmonies handed him by his accompanists, breaks up the continuity of the phrases, and rejects the received patterns that were current in his playing in the late '50s. The other players, however, do not benefit from this opening up of traditional structures; Rollins' innovations take place in front of, perhaps even depend on, a conventional accompaniment. Herbie Hancock, Jim Hall and Thad Jones also rarely get an opportunity to solo.

More than once, Rollins' love of experimentation, his rejection of the tried-and-true, becomes grotesque–for example, in the surreal saxophone coda to "I Remember Clifford," with its flute-like tone, or the tremulous, almost burlesque vibrato with which he renders the theme of John Lewis' "Django." The fact that these musical "alternatives" to *Now's The Time* and *The Standard Sonny Rollins* were kept under wraps for so long is not greatly surprising.

The 29 tracks in total represented here, all from the same seven-month period, in no way give a complete picture of Rollins' studio work of the time. Twelve more unreleased takes are indicated in Sjøgren's discography; presumably there are still others. Will RCA someday reopen the archives?

Sonny Rollins
There Will Never Be Another You
Impulse IA-9349
CD: Impulse IMP 12942
Sonny Rollins (ts) Tommy Flanagan (p) Bob Cranshaw (b) Mickey Roker, Billy Higgins (dr); New York, 6/17/65:
ON GREEN DOLPHIN STREET / THREE LITTLE WORDS / MADEMOISELLE DE PARIS / TO A WILD ROSE / THERE WILL NEVER BE ANOTHER YOU

Sonny Rollins in Paris
Jazzway LLM-1501
Sonny Rollins (ts) Gilbert Rovère (b) Art Taylor (dr); Paris (?), (1965):

I CAN'T GET STARTED / THREE LITTLE WORDS / I CAN'T GET STARTED / THREE LITTLE WORDS / ST. THOMAS / THERE WILL NEVER BE ANOTHER YOU / WHEN I GROW TOO OLD TO DREAM / MADEMOISELLE DE PARIS

It is no revelation that in jazz, not the "what" of the musical material, but the "how" of its execution is what matters. Still, this truth is pleasantly borne out by these two live recordings from 1965. The material is mostly familiar, and largely the same in both concerts: themes that Rollins had had in his concert repertoire for years. What is surprising and exciting, however, is the way Rollins the improviser continually rearranges the elements into new designs. This is what gives Rollins' appearances from these years their special quality. He does not program pieces conventionally, but jumps from one theme to the next, connecting or contrasting a dizzying amount of familiar material in long solo cadenzas. "Three Little Words," from the New York concert, changes mid-theme into "Mademoiselle de Paris"; "There Will Never Be Another You" (in which Rollins surprises his fellow musicians with a sudden modulation from G to E-flat) mutates by the end into a calypso.

Even more impressive is the recording from Paris, which was evidently made either in January or in fall of 1965 during one of Rollins' European tours that year. This recording, probably a radio broadcast that reached the Jazzway bootleggers through underground channels, is technically more satisfactory than the one made in the Museum of Modern Art sculpture garden. That recording was impaired by Rollins' need to move around; this one also has the advantage of completely documenting one of Rollins' free-association medleys, whereas the New York tape offers only excerpts. In a great 40-minute musical arc, Rollins jumps back and forth among the themes, returns repeatedly to a few thematic touchstones, and interpolates material ranging from "O Sole Mio" to "Cherokee" and his own "Pent-Up House." (The list of tracks above only partly and approximately represents this musical kaleidoscope.) Art Taylor, a childhood friend from the old Sugar Hill days, and French bassist Gilbert Rovère, prove responsive and inventive accompanists. Most fascinating, however, are Rollins' solo juggling acts, particularly at the end of the concert when he performs improvisations on "There Will Never Be Another You" for a quarter of an hour, with a dizzying multitude of citations, pseudo-citations, and a stream of associated motifs.

Sonny Rollins
On Impulse
Impulse! AS 91
CD: Impulse IMP 12232
Sonny Rollins (ts) Ray Bryant (p) Walter Booker (b) Mickey Roker (dr); Englewood Cliffs, 7/8/65:
ON GREEN DOLPHIN STREET / EVERYTHING HAPPENS TO ME / HOLD 'EM JOE / BLUE ROOM / THREE LITTLE WORDS

With his first studio production on the Impulse! label since 1958, Rollins was back in the studio as a guest of star sound engineer Rudy Van Gelder, who had meanwhile moved from Hackensack to Englewood Cliffs. Other things evoke the past as well, such as the participation of pianist Ray Bryant, a colleague from the days of the Max Roach Quintet, and the fact that a single studio date was enough to record the entire LP.

The repertoire is, in part, identical to the *There Will Never Be Another You* concert three weeks before. Musically, however, *On Impulse* is reminiscent of the last RCA albums (*Now's the Time!*) and (*The Standard Sonny Rollins*). The guiding principle, as liner-note writer Nat Hentoff so nicely puts it, is "exploring and elasticizing popular standards"—with a Rollins who is above all rhythmically creative, and a rhythm section that is exemplary in its liveliness and precise in its execution. With "Hold 'em Joe," Rollins adds another to his catalog of great calypso interpretations.

Sonny Rollins
Original Music From the Score *Alfie*
Impulse A/AS 9111
CD: Impulse IMP 12242
Sonny Rollins (ts) Jimmy Cleveland (tb) (on "Alfie's Theme Differently" J. J. Johnson replaces Jimmy Cleveland) Phil Woods (as) Bob Ashton (ts) Danny Bank (bs) Kenny Burrell (g) Roger Kellaway (p) Walter Booker (b) Frankie Dunlop (dr) Oliver Nelson (arr, cond); New York, 1/26/66:
ALFIE'S THEME / HE'S YOUNGER THAN YOU ARE / STREET RUNNER WITH CHILD / TRANSITION THEME FOR MINOR BLUES OR LITTLE MALCOLM LOVES HIS DAD / ON IMPULSE / ALFIE'S THEME DIFFERENTLY

"There's a lot of guys in England who can score films, so if they called me, I guess they want some distinctive music." Thus Sonny Rollins to Joe Goldberg (Goldberg 1965b, 21). And in fact, Rollins' music for the Lewis Gilbert film—with Michael Caine in the role that won him the Special Jury Award at Cannes in 1966—is anything but a typical orchestral film score.

How did the collaboration come about? The filmmakers approached Rollins during a guest spot at Ronnie Scott's in London, January 1965. Rollins agreed, but insisted on working closely and carefully with the director. He began to lay out the musical score only after having traveled to London again to see the finished film. A kind of music emerged that, while relating closely to the events and moods of the story regarding an aging Casanova, also maintains its artistic autonomy. Only in a few passages—for example, in the abruptly changing tempos of "Street Runner With Child"—does the programmatic material seem to call attention to itself. To illuminate the various situations, Rollins uses a wide range of styles: ballad ("He's Younger Than You Are"), jazz waltz ("On Impulse"), blues ("Transition Theme For Minor Blues"), up-tempo swing ("Street Runner With Child"). The most adaptable, however, is the simple "Alfie" theme, which functions as a kind of leitmotiv.

Not only in the composed parts (scored for a nine-piece ensemble with the help of Oliver Nelson) is Rollins faithful to the syntax of his own music (thereby avoiding the pompous symphonic pretensions typical of film music). At the heart of the music we also find Rollins the improviser—who does not pander to the cinematic audience, but instead lays out the whole range of his complex art as it had evolved up to 1966—the avant-garde Sonny Rollins, in fact, with all his harmonic, rhythmic, and tonal resources. The 10-minute-long "Alfie's Theme" is an especially wide-ranging example of Rollins' improvisational art (which still remains grounded in the melody).

Anyone hoping for solos by Phil Woods or by the two prominent horn players will be disappointed; apart from Rollins, only the guitar and piano share in the improvisations. The role of the orchestra is relatively modest; aside from the opening and closing themes it contributes mostly simple background music.

Sonny Rollins
East Broadway Run Down
Impulse A/AS 9121
Sonny Rollins (ts) Freddie Hubbard (tp on "East Broadway Run Down") Jimmy Garrison (b) Elvin Jones (dr); New York, 5/9/66:
EAST BROADWAY RUN DOWN / BLESSING IN DISGUISE / WE KISS IN A SHADOW

Elvin Jones and Jimmy Garrison formed one of the great rhythm sections in modern jazz. For four years, from the end of 1961 to the end of 1965, the drummer and bassist had played together in John Coltrane's quartet, and had contributed decisively to the group's powerful, polyrhythmic sound. Their collaboration with Sonny Rollins–who, unlike Coltrane, was a rhythmic virtuoso–promised a lot. In terms of passion and rhythmic tension, *East Broadway Run Down* fulfills those expectations.

Still, the music has its flaws. The spontaneity of this one-time meeting is counterbalanced by a certain rawness in the group dynamic. The Latin rhythm of the musical theme "We Kiss in a Shadow" seems tentative, at times unsteady. In addition, the 20-minute title track (the only one to which Freddie Hubbard contributes) is more patchwork than musical whole. The brief opening theme–a short off-beat figure that gets a little longer with every repetition–segues directly into a blues that both horn soloists handle freely. The subsequent bass and drum solos disrupt the group playing, which recovers only with effort, and without clear direction. "Blessing In Disguise" is better defined. A common riff (which, as Arrigo Polillo believes, may indeed have lifted from Lionel Hampton's hit "Hey-ba-ba-re-bop" (Polillo 1981, 564) is the starting point and anchor for a seemingly endless chain of rhythmically and thematically ingenious refinements, played over a sequence of two harmonies performed *ostinato*.

East Broadway Run Down is an inspired, but unfinished document of a meeting that many wished could have been the start of a longer association. Instead, it marked the beginning of the longest break in Sonny Rollins' recording career, lasting six years.

Sonny Rollins
Next Album

Milestone MSP-9042 (Original Jazz Classics OJC-312)
CD: Original Jazz Classics OJCCD 312-2
Sonny Rollins (ts, ss) George Cables (p, e-p) Bob Cranshaw (b, e-b) Jack DeJohnette (dr) Arthur Jenkins (perc on "Playin' In The Yard"); New York, 7/14/72:
PLAYIN' IN THE YARD / KEEP HOLD OF YOURSELF
Same personnel but David Lee replaces Jack DeJohnette; New York, 7/27/72:
POINCIANA / THE EVERYWHERE CALYPSO / SKYLARK

After a six-year-long recording break, Rollins' laconically titled *Next Album* was awaited with particular excitement, comparable to that of *The Bridge*. If in 1962 there had been mild

disappointment at not hearing a "new" Rollins, this time the critics' voices were subdued in their enthusiasm as well—but for opposite reasons. Now it was too much new that annoyed them.

With the first bars of "Playin' In the Yard," the signs of the times are evident. Rollins plays a riff-like melody over a heavy backbeat, accompanied by electric bass and piano, that snugly fits into the fusion soundscape. His subsequent solo remains squarely, even timorously tied to the rock beat and simple harmony. (Jack DeJohnette does a better job of demonstrating how to play interestingly within the limited parameters of this music.) There is no doubt about it: this Sonny Rollins is worlds away from the saxophone player of the same name on *East Broadway Run Down.*

It is not the choice of material *per se* that makes *Next Album* problematic. Rollins had always been eclectic in his choice of material; he had never shied away from what was popular, or from themes atypical of jazz. But he had always transcended dubious material with his improvisation, making the music unmistakably his own. This sort of personalization is hardly in evidence here. While on "Playin' in the Yard" Rollins sounds like an average rhythm-and-blues saxophone player, in the minor blues "Keep Hold of Yourself" he is a carbon copy of the John Coltrane of the modal years, pentatonic clichés and all. The Latin track "Poinciana" also evokes Coltrane–inevitably, since Rollins is heard here for the first time on the soprano saxophone. (In the process, he cannot avoid several intonation problems typical of sopranos.) "Everywhere Calypso," on the other hand, should be–judging from its theme–Rollins at his best, yet even on this familiar ground the saxophone player comes far short of his own standards, both in rhythmic and harmonic invention. Ironically, it is only on the most stylistically retro track–the ballad "Skylark," with prolonged unaccompanied passages–that Rollins does himself justice.

Sonny Rollins
Horn Culture

Milestone M-9051 (Original Jazz Classics OJC-314)
CD: Original Jazz Classics OJCCD 314-2

Sonny Rollins (ts, ss) Yoshiaki Masuo (g) Walter Davis, Jr. (p, e-p) Bob Cranshaw (e-b) David Lee (dr) James Mtume (perc, p on "Saïs"); New York and Berkeley, April, June, and July 1973:
PICTURES IN THE REFLECTION OF A GOLDEN HORN / SAÏS / NOTES FOR EDDIE / GOD BLESS THE CHILD / LOVE MAN / GOOD MORNING, HEARTACHE

The confluence of bop past and fusion present continues on *Horn Culture*, with scarcely better results. Rollins' own compositions–two blues tracks ("Notes For Eddie" and "Love Man") and a modal riff ("Pictures in the Reflection of a Golden Horn") are uninspiring and only generate an interchangeable series of modal, especially pentatonic, clichés found on too many other record productions of the time. The same goes for Mtume's *ostinato* piece "Saïs," which does create some interesting, orchestral textures with its synchronicity of piano and electric piano while Rollins adds expressive tonal explorations in his soprano overdubs. His experiments with overdubbing, heard here for the first time, are further exploited on the first two tracks, where the saxophonist plays a duet with himself–perhaps because he cannot find an equal partner among his fellow musicians; the act of talking to himself acts as a substitute for group interaction.

Saddest of all, though, is that Rollins fails on the two ballads from Billie Holiday's repertoire to attain the heights of earlier performances. On "God Bless the Child," known from the legendary 1962 *Bridge* LP, only the magisterial presentation of the theme impresses. "Good Morning, Heartache" suffers not only from tuning problems among the string instruments, but also from the fact that the piece was clearly put together from two different takes.

Sonny Rollins in Japan
JVC CD4W-7059E (Victor-SMJ 6030 / G.I. GSS 4)
CD: Victor VICJ 23001
Sonny Rollins (ts) Yoshiaki Masuo (g) Bob Cranshaw (e-b) David Lee (dr) James Mtume (perc); Tokyo, 9/30/73:
POWAII / ST. THOMAS / ALFIE'S THEME / MORITAT

Sonny Rollins
The Cutting Edge
Milestone M-9059 (Original Jazz Classics OJC-468)
CD: Original Jazz Classics OJCCD 468-2
Personnel as above plus Stanley Cowell (p on "Swing Low, Sweet Chariot") Rufus Harley (bagpipes); Montreux, 6/6/74:
THE CUTTING EDGE / TO A WILD ROSE / FIRST MOVES / A HOUSE IS NOT A HOME / SWING LOW, SWEET CHARIOT

If one cites the Milestone LPs of the '70s as evidence of an artistic crisis, Rollins fans will be quick to counter with enthusiastic descriptions of his contemporary live appearances. The studio releases of these years, it is often argued, are a mere shadow of his artistic potential. Two live recordings of a formation that more or less matches the ensemble on *Horn*

Culture are fertile grounds to test this theory. The results are equivocal. There are in fact some tracks on the two albums that prove Rollins apologists right. One is an intimate, relaxed reading of the Edward McDowell salon piano piece "To a Wild Rose," with a wonderfully constructed solo cadenza, the other is an "Alfie's Theme" that does manage to compensate for some of Rollins' timid studio solos from this period. It shows us a Sonny Rollins on a playing high, overflowing with ideas from the passionate start. And this is a Sonny who is not just energized, but also shows his intellectual virtuosity through many nuances of articulation, the switching of tempos, and the bold expansion and compression of the theme material. On the other hand, there are pieces that only exacerbate the faults of the studio records, as the long tracks only serve to expose them more mercilessly. The 19-minute "Powaii" is one example: a noisy, incoherent rhythm section supports overlong improvisations, caught up in familiar modal patterns played over an unvarying tonal center. (The same applies to "The Cutting Edge" and "First Moves" on the Montreux Festival recording.) The same appearance as "Powaii," however–in the Nakano Sun Plaza in Tokyo–produced an inspired "Moritat," a substantial (if unremarkable) "St. Thomas," and the splendid "Alfie's Theme" mentioned above.

What conclusion can we draw? Probably only this: that Sonny Rollins the live performer could be just as erratic as Sonny Rollins in the studio.

Sonny Rollins
Nucleus
Milestone M-9064 (Original Jazz Classics OJC-620)
CD: Original Jazz Classics OJCCD-620-2
Sonny Rollins (ts) Bennie Maupin (ss, bcl, lyricon) Raul de Souza (tb) George Duke (p, e-p, synth) David Amaro, Blackbird McKnight (g) Bob Cranshaw (e-b on "Newkleus," "My Reverie," and "Azalea") Chuck Rainey (e-b on remaining titles) Roy McCurdy (dr on tracks with Cranshaw) Eddie Moore (dr on tracks with Rainey) James Mtume (perc, g on "Newkleus"); Berkeley, 9/2–5/75:
LUCILLE / GWALIGO / ARE YOU READY? / AZALEA / NEWKLEUS / COSMET / MY REVERIE

Rollins did more writing to prepare for *Nucleus* than he had for his previous Milestone albums. Five of the seven tracks are premieres of his own pieces, and alongside simple riff numbers there are more originally and elaborately constructed themes like the 20-bar "Are You Ready?" and the AABA-form "Azalea," with its B section lengthened to 12 bars.

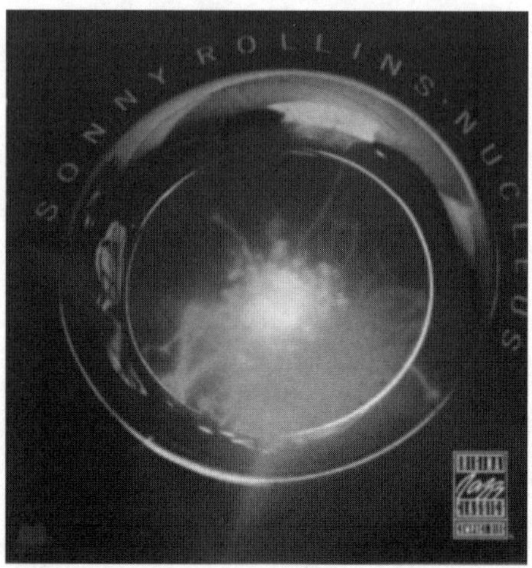

Still, the overall impression is similar to, and no more positive than, the other post-comeback LPs: a few bop-oriented tracks ("Cosmet," "Azalea"), on which Rollins the master improviser shines, are countered by fusion tracks based on static, all-too-simple riffs that appear to hobble Rollins' creativity as a soloist. (This might also be due to the overly elaborate rhythm section of up to six musicians.) Musical ingredients popular at the time–distorted guitars, lyricon and synthesizer sounds–make this album seem, in retrospect, more of a period piece than many Rollins recordings from the '50s and '60s. Rollins' saxophone sound is tonally complex, but for the first time has a persistent rough edge even on the ballad "My Reverie."

Sonny Rollins
The Way I Feel
Milestone M-9074

Sonny Rollins (ts) Lee Ritenour (g) Patrice Rushen (p, e-p, synth) Alex Blake (b, e-b on "Love Reborn," "The Way I Feel About You," and "Charm Baby") Charles Meeks (e-b on remaining tracks) Billy Cobham (dr) Bill Summers (perc); Berkeley, August and October 1976:
ISLAND LADY / ASFRANTATION WOOGIE / LOVE REBORN / HAPPY FEEL / SHOUT IT OUT / THE WAY I FEEL ABOUT YOU / CHARM BABY

The Way I Feel involves more compromises than the other Milestone albums–or fewer, depending on your perspective. It is an unabashedly commercial production, without the stylistic leaps of the previous productions, without even a sop for Rollins purists (even the production, with its horn charts added later, is adapted to the lucrative fusion trend). Rollins is entirely on the terrain of soul-sax matadors like Junior Walker or Grover Washington, Jr. One could regret this–but at the same time will have to admit that these seven pieces are more successful, in their way, than most of the earlier fusion pieces by and featuring Rollins. The rhythm section is tighter and better integrated, and the catchy if hardly memorable four-and eight-bar themes, instead of sticking with a single harmony, make use of small "turnarounds." Both of these are more congenial to Rollins' personality as a soloist than the sometimes crude, uncomplicated harmonies on previous records, and his playing seems significantly more relaxed and self-assured as a result. "Easy listening" then, with Sonny Rollins. Still, it cannot be denied that Rollins is playing leagues below his level of expertise, and that Junior Walker and Grover Washington, Jr. simply have more facility at this game.

Sonny Rollins
Easy Living
Milestone M-9080
CD: Original Jazz Classics OJCCD 893-2
Sonny Rollins (ts, ss) Charles Icarus Johnson (g) George Duke (p, e-p) Byron Miller (e-b on "Isn't She Lovely") Paul Jackson (e-b on remaining tracks) Tony Williams (dr) Bill Summers (perc on "Isn't She Lovely"); Berkeley, 8/3–6/77:
ISN'T SHE LOVELY / DOWN THE LINE / MY ONE AND ONLY LOVE / ARROZ CON POLLO / EASY LIVING / HEAR WHAT I'M SAYING

Those Rollins fans who thought that with *The Way I Feel* their idol had sold out for good, could breathe a sigh of relief with *Easy Living.* The record does not exactly mark a return to the good old days, but it is at least a return to the stylistic complexity of Rollins' first Milestone albums. It includes ballads,

bop, and pop—although the last is only represented here by the successful Stevie Wonder adaptation "Isn't She Lovely" and the somewhat simple-minded Latin number "Arroz con Pollo." With "Down the Line," on the other hand, after all the trite riff tunes of the recent records, a piece that is structurally interesting as well can be heard; nine-bar A sections are followed by B sections whose length the soloist can re-determine every time, on the principle of Mingus' "extended form." Themes like this and the 32-bar "Hear What I'm Saying" inspire Rollins to eloquent improvisations—and in "Down The Line" it results in an (unfortunately too-brief) interplay between Rollins and Tony Williams (whose vibrant drumming—nervous but in a good way—is regrettably sabotaged by poor recording equipment). The most interesting numbers, however, are the ballads; while Rollins delivers his most successful soprano saxophone performance to date on "My One and

Only Love," helped by a wonderfully warm tone, the title piece surprises with its melancholy tenor sound, varied tone, and abrupt leaps into "energy playing." The sum of all these qualities made *Easy Living* Rollins' most compelling Milestone LP up to then.

Sonny Rollins
Don't Stop the Carnival
Milestone M-55005
CD: Milestone MCD 55005-2
Sonny Rollins (ts) Donald Byrd (tp, flh [not on the first four tracks]) Aurell Ray (g) Mark Soskin (p, e-p) Jerry Harris (e-b) Tony Williams (dr); San Francisco, 4/13–15/78:
DON'T STOP THE CARNIVAL / SILVER CITY/ AUTUMN NOCTURNE / CAMEL / NOBODY ELSE BUT ME / NON-CENTS / A CHILD'S PRAYER / PRESIDENT HAYES / SAÏS

On the first four tracks of this recording from the Great American Music Hall, Rollins offers up his concert blend, characteristic even today, of calypso ("Don't Stop the Carnival"), ballad ("Autumn Nocturne"), medium swing ("Silver City") and fusion ("Camel"). In the title track, he and Tony Williams drive each other on to increasingly euphoric heights, culminating in ecstatic "energy playing." In the 20-bar-structured "Silver City," theme-oriented passages alternate with radically free ones, and "Autumn Nocturne"—up until the final chorus, which is played by the ensemble—is a solo improvisation that is spun out in a wonderfully wide and unfettered way, full of quotations and allusions.

So far so good. If only it weren't for Donald Byrd, Rollins' "very special friend" (according to the cover) and companion from the early Blue Note days. When he joins in, the music degenerates into fusion banality. His themes, alternating between funk formulas and sentimental mush, don't help, nor do his faceless improvisations. Even Tony Williams sags here. Gary Giddins described this double LP as Rollins' most disappointing, despite its high points, and one can understand why: the high and low points are so extreme, and so close together (Giddins 1981, 124).

Here for the first time pianist Mark Soskin and bass player Jerome (Jerry) Harris can be heard with Rollins–two musicians the usually fickle saxophonist worked with, onstage and in the studio, for over a decade.

Milestone Jazz Stars in Concert
Milestone M-55006
CD: Milestone MCD-55006-2
Sonny Rollins (ts, ss) McCoy Tyner (p) Ron Carter (b), Al Foster (dr); San Francisco, Madison, New Haven; September–October 1978:
THE CUTTING EDGE / CONTINUUM / NUBIA / N.O. BLUES / IN A SENTIMENTAL MOOD / DON'T STOP THE CARNIVAL
(Three or two (CD) additional tracks without Rollins)

Forming a group based on the fact that the members all record for the same label–the idea could only have originated with a record producer. From a musical standpoint, at least, it was a strange group that completed a 20-concert tour of the United States between September 16 and October 29, 1978. Rollins

had worked with bassist Carter in 1964, with good results; on the other hand, he had never played with McCoy Tyner, and probably never would have had it not been for Milestone producer Orrin Keepnews. Tyner, whose playing is anything but restrained, hardly seemed the right partner for a saxophonist who constantly felt oppressed by pianists who played too densely and assertively.

The Tyner composition "Nubia" feeds these misgivings; when faced with Tyner's massive chord structures and cascades, Rollins (here playing soprano sax) appears to be at a loss. But on other tracks, he reaches a surprisingly amicable working relationship with his costars. "The Cutting Edge" seems more solid in this quartet setting than the feeble Montreux version of 1974, and it offers a considerably looser, harmonically more adventurous saxophone solo than the first recording. Ron Carter's "N.O. Blues"—the title reflects the fact that it is a regular blues only in feeling and not as regards the 20-bar form–inspires Rollins to a rhythmically gripping improvisation, with strong rhythm-and-blues elements. Rollins finally manages here to match the intensity of a Junior Walker or King Curtis that he had strived for in vain on previous records. While the (pianoless) trio version of "Don't Stop The Carnival" is clearly inferior to the recording made in April of the same year–especially as regards the interplay between saxophone and drums–the duo with Tyner on Ellington's "In a Sentimental Mood" works well despite the pianist's orchestral approach. "Continuum" delivers another valuable demonstration of the continuity of theme and improvisation in Rollins' solo excursions.

Sonny Rollins
Don't Ask
Milestone M-9090
CD: Original Jazz Classics OJCCD 955-2
Sonny Rollins (ts) Larry Coryell (g); Berkeley 5/15–18/79:
THE FILE / MY IDEAL
Same location, same dates, plus Mark Soskin (p, e-p, synth) Jerome Harris (e-b) Al Foster (b) Bill Summers (perc):
HARLEM BOYS / DISCO MONK / DON'T ASK / TAI-CHI / AND THEN MY LOVE I FOUND YOU

Don't Ask, once again conceived in the now-familiar Milestone mold, falls below the standard of *Easy Living.* The idea of enlivening a combo production with duo passages has merit–but Larry Coryell is the wrong partner for it. "The File" (a pure duet), with its hectic guitar playing, sounds like a piece that is missing a rhythm section–a sure sign the duet idea has failed.

In "My Ideal," too, no real duo interaction is achieved. The piece is de facto a sequence of two a cappella solos–and Rollins' wonderful unaccompanied chorus raises the question why he didn't just record the ballad by himself. Rollins' own compositions prove to be either predictable (the 32-bar AABA swing tracks "Don't Ask" and "And Then My Love I Found You"), or errors in taste. The penetrating disco beat on "Disco Monk"–relieved by equally clichéd ballad passages–makes one hope that it is not Rollins' mentor Thelonious Monk, even in his lifetime, who is being so dubiously "honored." "Tai-Chi" is pure Eastern kitsch that omits no Asian musical cliché–from Rollins' high, melismatic lyricon (its debut on record), meant to suggest an Asian flute, to the obligatory fifth and fourth parallels on the piano.

Sonny Rollins
Love At First Sight

Milestone M-9098
CD: Original Jazz Classics OJCCD 753-2
Sonny Rollins (ts, lyricon on "The Dream That We Fell Out Of") George Duke (p, e-p) Stanley Clarke (e-b) Al Foster (dr) Bill Summers (perc on "Little Lu," "Strode Rode," and "Caress"); Berkeley, 5/9–12/80:
LITTLE LU / THE DREAM THAT WE FELL OUT OF / STRODE RODE / THE VERY THOUGHT OF YOU / CARESS / DOUBLE FEATURE

Love At First Sight is a record without any particular high points. One the one hand, it does not pander too much to the putative tastes of the masses; on the other, it contains little that would make fans of the "old" Rollins happy. "Strode Rode" does hark back to *Saxophone Colossus* from 1956, but only makes the vital first recording shine more brightly by comparison. (It is worth mentioning that Rollins interprets the piece, originally in F minor, in D minor now). "Little Lu," Rollins' only new composition on the album, is no more substantial than the contributions of Stanley Clarke ("The Dream That We Fell Out Of," with synthetic lyricon schmaltz) and George Duke ("Caress"). Even the obligatory ballad–Ray Noble's "The Very Thought Of You"–does not furnish the creative stimulus that it does on so many other Milestone LPs. Rollins' ideas remain fragmentary, and his tenor sound–as throughout the record–seems strangely pale and lusterless. Most regrettable, perhaps, is the fact that Rollins plods even in the terrain of his former brilliant achievements: on the blues "Double Feature," played as a duet with Clarke, he is caught up in tired clichés.

Sonny Rollins
No Problem
Milestone M-9104
CD: Original Jazz Classics OJCCD 1014-2
Sonny Rollins (ts) Bobby Broom (g) Bobby Hutcherson (vib) Bob Cranshaw (e-b) Tony Williams (dr); Berkeley, 12/9–15/81:
NO PROBLEM / HERE YOU COME AGAIN / JO JO / COCONUT BREAD / PENNY SAVED / ILLUSIONS / JOYOUS LAKE

Often, the high points in Rollins' music occur where they are least expected. It is not the calypso "Coconut Bread" that shows us Rollins at his most inspired, not the innocent Latin title track, not "Joyous Lake"–composed in an original 25-bar AABA form (4+4+9+8)–not even the obligatory ballad.

No, instead it is on the Dolly Parton hit "Here You Come

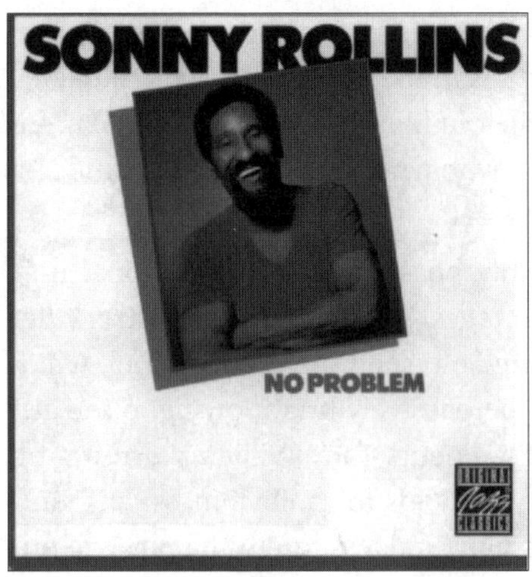

Again" that Rollins works his old magic. An everyday hit becomes an improvisational triumph through Rollins' inexhaustible creativity with the motifs, and his lively, bravura articulation. (What is surprising here is the way Rollins revives the percussive staccato articulation of his '50s recordings–and, tonally speaking, sounds just like the Rollins from the pre-Bridge period.) As heretical as it might sound, perhaps the Parton number was more melodically fertile than the material contributed by Rollins, Bobby Broome ("Penny Saved") and Bobby Hutcherson ("Jo Jo"). According to Rollins: "That one I've always liked a lot, from the minute I heard it on the radio. I think that we hear songs in their complete form–melody, harmony, rhythm, lyrics–but of course, playing a horn, I guess I'm drawn to a melody line at first." (Cioe 1983, 77). The choice of "Illusions," on the other hand–the ballad mentioned earlier, which unfortunately can only be heard in a somewhat lackluster two-minute version–goes back to much earlier experiences, as Rollins reports in the same interview: "'Illusions' is from one of my favorite old films, *A Foreign Affair*. Marlene Dietrich sang it. The guy who wrote it, Friedrich Hollander, is one of my favorite composers."

Even if *No Problem* only boasts one improvisational high point, it has other advantages. There is no synthesizer filler, no synthetic lyricon sounds to spoil the group sound, which is both transparent and percussively bright owing to the guitar and vibraphone in the lineup. Tony Williams' drumming, both swinging and forceful, adds to the liveliness; and Rollins' saxophone, more radiant and less rough than on the previous records, is well recorded–not something to be taken for granted.

The sum of these qualities makes *No Problem* one of the more pleasing records in the characteristic Milestone format–which remained the same even though the producer was no longer Orrin Keepnews, but Sonny Rollins (with Lucille Rollins as co-producer).

Rolling Stones
Tattoo You
Rolling Stones Record/EMI 1C 064-64 533
Mick Jagger (voc, g) Keith Richard (g) Ron Wood (key) Bill Wyman (e-b) Charlie Watts (dr) Sonny Rollins (ts) unidentified choir; Nassau/Bahamas and Paris, 1981:
SLAVE / NEIGHBOURS / WAITING ON A FRIEND
(Eight additional tracks without Rollins)

The impetus for this, probably the least reputable item in

Rollins' discography, was an appearance at the Bottom Line in New York. Mick Jagger, who was in the audience, was so taken with Rollins' performance that he asked him to contribute to the Rolling Stones' next LP. Rollins' possible motives for accepting the curious offer have already been discussed in the chapter about his personality. For the Stones it does, in fact, seem to have been about music rather than business. They did not exploit the publicity benefits of Rollins' involvement and his name is not listed on the cover. (Rollins' comment: "It doesn't bother me. In fact, since I was worried about how I sounded, I'm glad I didn't get a credit." (Blumenthal 1982, 17)

Rollins' solos and fills, mixed into the rhythm tracks, and recorded, he says, together with Jagger's vocals, were certainly well paid for, but, he adds, involved a lot of effort: "It was hard–I had to do a lot of takes and really get with the stuff, you know. It was real work, just like anything else I'd do, and I took it just as seriously–definitely not something to slough off." (Cioe 1983, 90)

Rollins' commitment to the project is evident in his contributions: depending on the musical context, he provides a rich palette of tonal and rhythmic nuances, from the relaxed fill-in phrase to the raw falsetto shriek. The contrast with the Stones' instrumental efforts, which seem amateurish by comparison–Charlie Watts' wooden drumming especially–gives this collaboration an odd character at times.

Sonny Rollins
Reel Life
Milestone M-9108

Sonny Rollins (ts) Bobby Broom, Yoshiaki Masuo (g) Bob Cranshaw (e-b) Jack DeJohnette (dr); Berkeley, 8/17–22/82:
REEL LIFE / MCGHEE / ROSITA'S BEST FRIEND / SONNY SIDE UP / MY LITTLE BROWN BOOK / BEST WISHES / SOLO REPRISE (SONNY)

"I wanted to do it as a 'live' jazz album in the studio–I think the only overdub was the guitar solo. I was very comfortable with the band since we'd been working together live for some time... I knew the line-up would change after the album..., and I really wanted to make a statement of our work together." (Cioe 1983, 77) It is a worthy ambition that Rollins, as producer, expresses here. Unfortunately, the results do not live up to it. There is little evidence of mutual stimulation, or the ebullience of a concert setting. This might be due to the banal material in this typical Milestone mix ("Rosita's Best Friend," for example, is one of Rollins' dullest calypso inspirations). Only the blues "McGhee," which (as Rollins reveals in the interview quoted above) is based on a trumpet line by Howard McGhee from a long-ago date together, yields a more-than-routine improvisation. Not once does the "Solo Reprise" reach the level of other Rollins solo outings. It seems to be a gratuitous afterthought, and, furthermore, the recording is a technical failure; even on his worst days Rollins surely never sounded this thin and insubstantial.

Sonny Rollins
Sunny Days, Starry Nights
Milestone M-9122
CD: Fantasy FCD 604-9122
Sonny Rollins (ts) Clifton Anderson (tb) Mark Soskin (p, e-p,

synth, celesta) Russel Blake (e-b) Tommy Campbell (dr); Berkeley, 1/23–27/84:
MAVA MAVA / I'M OLD FASHIONED / WYNTON / TELL ME YOU LOVE ME / I'LL SEE YOU AGAIN / KILAUEA

"*Sunny Days and Starry Nights* [sic] is the first Rollins LP in ages that one can enjoy from start to finish without first scaling down one's expectations." (Davis 1986, 129) Indeed, this is the first of Rollins' Milestone records that succeeds in transferring the energy of his live performances, undiminished, into the studio–the freedom and vivacity, the humor, the rhythmic and harmonic daring, one might even say the recklessness. Rollins evokes the most euphoric of his "St. Thomas" and "Don't Stop The Carnival" interpretations on no fewer than three calypso tracks–"Mava Mava," "Tell Me You Love Me," and "Kilauea." "I'm Old Fashioned," Rollins confesses–not without a certain irony, since his choruses, skillfully making bold melodic and harmonic detours and just as skillfully returning to solid ground, prove the opposite. Even the studio equipment, which failed him on several earlier Milestone LPs, makes itself useful for once, when two tenor saxophone players by the name of Sonny Rollins annotate and counterpoint each others' lines on the sentimental old Noel Coward number "I'll See You Again."

Clifton Anderson's full trombone sound complements well the tenor's bristly tone in the presentation of the themes. Rollins' nephew has little to add in the way of solos, however, and pianist Mark Soskin, whose trenchant playing is well adapted to the ensemble sound, fares no better in this respect. The hierarchy of leader and sidemen is clearer than ever, though this will hardly be seen as a drawback. The bass-percussion team, with whom Rollins is clearly comfortable, is precise and impressive, though their sound is rather hard.

In summary: this record delivers what every Rollins record since the *Next Album* of 1972 had promised, but failed to provide–an up-to-the-minute Sonny Rollins who remains true to himself. The record's success has something to do with a new approach to studio work, reminiscent of Miles Davis, as the following remarks by Rollins indicate: "We use a rather costly procedure which involves just letting the tape run and not marking every take separately. Sometimes we let the tape roll while we practice. This way the music sounds less rehearsed and more natural. That's what we did for the first time with the *Sunny Days, Starry Nights* record. Sometimes my sidemen forgot that they were being recorded. Sometimes *I* forgot we were being recorded." (Kalbacher 1988, 19)

Sonny Rollins
The Solo Album
Milestone M-9137
Sonny Rollins (ts); New York, 7/19/85:
SOLOSCOPE (PART I) / SOLOSCOPE (PART 2)

"My ultimate goal is unaccompanied tenor. I've been working toward this a long time. I'm convinced I've still got a long way to go. But I'm sure it can be done. I want to go on a concert stage and render a solo...a solo on the tenor. Like Segovia does on the guitar." Thus Sonny Rollins, in a conversation with Dom Cerulli appearing in *Down Beat* on July 10, 1958. Rollins had attempted an unaccompanied solo the year before ("It Could Happen to You" on *The Sound of Sonny*); there had been unaccompanied saxophone solos on many of his live and studio recordings since then. Still, it would be some time before his ambition would be fully realized. About 1966 (as Rollins recalls), he gave his first solo concert in Berkeley, Cali-

fornia (Kalbacher 1988, 18). In 1969, he appeared alone at the Whitney Museum in New York, in the context of a "Composers' Showcase" concert (Williams 1969, 37). But it was not until 1985 that a complete solo outing was recorded for album release.

The concert—like the 1965 appearance recorded by Impulse—took place in the sculpture garden of the Museum of Modern Art in New York. Rollins had thought a little bit about the style of his presentation, but had left the final decision up to the mood of the moment: "I had several options. I had considered sitting down and playing the whole thing; I had some [sheet] music and themes I'd sketched out, but I didn't refer to them. Or I figured I might stand up and play while I walked around, and that's what I ended up doing. The excitement in the air led to my being more forceful and walking around." (Kalbacher 1988, 18) (Rollins' need for movement also required him to attach a microphone to his instrument, resulting in distracting valve sounds and excessively loud, distorted notes in the low register).

In 1958, the idea of a solo saxophone concert was radically new. Coleman Hawkins' unaccompanied "Picasso" solo of 1948 was an anomaly. In 1985 it was different; the unaccompanied horn solo had already been essayed from different angles in Anthony Braxton's 1968 *For Alto* recordings, and in Roscoe Mitchell and Steve Lacy's solo programs. However, Rollins did not model his concert on those precedents. Braxton and Mitchell planned their improvisations as systematic explorations of particular playing techniques and textures, and Steve Lacy worked with predetermined material—themes by

Thelonious Monk. Rollins' unaccompanied performance, on the other hand (as indicated by the title "Soloscope"), is a kaleidoscope of completely heterogeneous material, in the tradition of his solo cadenzas. From originals like "Alfie's Theme" and "St. Thomas," standards like "Mr. P.C." and "Tune Up," Broadway melodies like "There's No Business Like Show Business," through classical and semi-classical selections like Edward McDowell's "To a Wild Rose" and Prokofiev's "Peter and The Wolf," all the way through to marches, folk songs and pop songs ("I'll Never Fall in Love Again"), a broad spectrum of styles and genres unfolds in a continuous stream of association.

Still, an hour-long, one-man concert is different from a three- or five-minute solo flourish: the question of form inevitably arises, and Rollins–despite his virtuosity, his humor, his idiosyncratic eclecticism–has no prepared solution. In the course of the five "segments" into which "Soloscope" is divided (and whose character hardly diverges one from another), the flow of the music, the logic of the motifs, and the association of quotes run together, and all too often scale passages are needed to make the fragile construction cohere. In addition, the whole thing gives an impression of haste and breathlessness–as if Rollins were giving himself and the audience no pause, failing to make use of the musical rest as a means to impose order and create tension. The finale, where Rollins' rollicking riff inspires the audience to clap along, provides a jubilant ending–but only momentarily glosses over the concert's musical problems.

Asked about *The Solo Album* in the *Down Beat* interview,

Rollins remarks self-critically, "I have listened to it, but there's so much I am displeased with. In fact, I want to do another solo album." When the reporter reminds Rollins that he said he would never make another one, Rollins is equivocal: "I've done a lot of solo playing, and that album, whatever its faults or merits, did not in my estimation catch me when I'm really doing it. No, I don't want to do another one, but...to make a record I can live with, I've considered doing another one."

Sonny Rollins
G-Man

Milestone M-9150
CD: Milestone MCD 9150-2
Sonny Rollins (ts) Clifton Anderson (tb) Mark Soskin (p) Bob Cranshaw (e-b) Marvin "Smitty" Smith (dr); Saugerties, N.Y, 8/16/86; saxophone overdubs on "Kim," New York, 4/9/87:
G-MAN / KIM / DON'T STOP THE CARNIVAL / TENOR MADNESS (only CD)

A Rollins Quintet concert was recorded in August 1986 for the soundtrack of Robert Mugge's film portrait *Saxophone Colossus*–the first live album of a Rollins combo since 1978 (*Don't Stop the Carnival*). Rollins himself was just as dissatisfied with this production as he was with the *Solo Album* of the previous year: "I haven't listened to that since I mixed it. I wasn't doing what I wanted to do exactly... That record has been very well received, I think, but I can't listen to it." (Kalbacher 1988, 18)

Even allowing for Rollins' perpetual dissatisfaction, several weaknesses of *G-Man* can't be ignored. The title track–15 minutes of unadulterated Rollins–shows once again that

modal improvisation is not the saxophonist's strong point. Too many modal, especially pentatonic, formulas make this study in the key of G a somewhat tedious listen. The familiar old calypso "Don't Stop the Carnival" also contains *longueurs* side by side with inspired passages, though Marvin "Smitty" Smith's lively and communicative drumming compensates somewhat. The structurally irregular Rollins original "Kim" (with six-bar A sections in an AABA form), and the blues "Tenor Madness," finally give Clifton Anderson and Mark Soskin a chance to show off their solo potential. The pianist in particular shines, with his melodically inventive, clearly articulated choruses from the Tommy Flanagan school. The last track is only on the CD edition–added to eke out the meager 32-minute playing time.

Sonny Rollins
Dancing In the Dark

Milestone M-9155
CD: Milestone MCD-9155-2
Sonny Rollins (ts) Clifton Anderson (tb) Mark Soskin (p, e-p) Jerome Harris (e-b, g on "I'll String Along With You") Marvin "Smitty" Smith (dr); Berkeley, 9/15–25/87:
JUST ONCE / O.T.Y.O.G. / PROMISE / DUKE OF IRON / DANCING IN THE DARK / I'LL STRING ALONG WITH YOU / ALLISON / ALLISON (alternative take, only CD)

On *Dancing in the Dark,* Sonny Rollins has assembled his best studio lineup in a long time. Clifton Anderson and Mark Soskin, capable if not outstanding soloists, once again prove themselves to be natural group-oriented players. Marvin "Smitty" Smith unites refined yet powerful drumming with an unusual sensitivity to the different genres of Rollins' eclectic repertoire, and Jerome Harris–last heard with Rollins on *Don't Ask* (1979)–is an exceptionally clear and melodic soloist and accompanist on the electric bass.

Despite these conditions, the record only occasionally attains the heights of *Sunny Days, Starry Nights.* Rollins, as so often in the studio, seems inhibited and tentative, at least on the first three tracks. The calypso "Duke of Iron"—according to Rollins, named for a legendary 1930s singer from Trinidad—loosens things up, but Rollins does not really play freely until the title track. Starting with the enthusiastic a cappella introduction, Rollins shows that he wants to use the old, schmaltzy Broadway tune as a starting point for wide-ranging arabesques that touch on the thematic material only in passing. Unfortunately, this particular flight of fancy is spoiled by a pinched saxophone sound interrupted by rattling noises, a result of having a miniature microphone attached directly to the bell of the instrument, as on *Solo Album* and *G-Man.* This gives the saxophonist his desired freedom of movement, but at some cost to his tone. A second track also illustrates the unorthodox approach to standards, but in a completely different way: a reggae groove is laid under "I'll String Along with You"—Harris contributes a stylistically confident rhythm guitar—and Rollins once again demonstrates his affinity for Caribbean rhythms.

Sonny Rollins
Falling in Love with Jazz
Milestone M-9179
CD: Milestone CDMX 9179
Sonny Rollins, Branford Marsalis (ts) Tommy Flanagan (p) Jerome Harris (e-b) Jeff Watts (dr); New York, 6/3/89:
FOR ALL WE KNOW / I SHOULD CARE

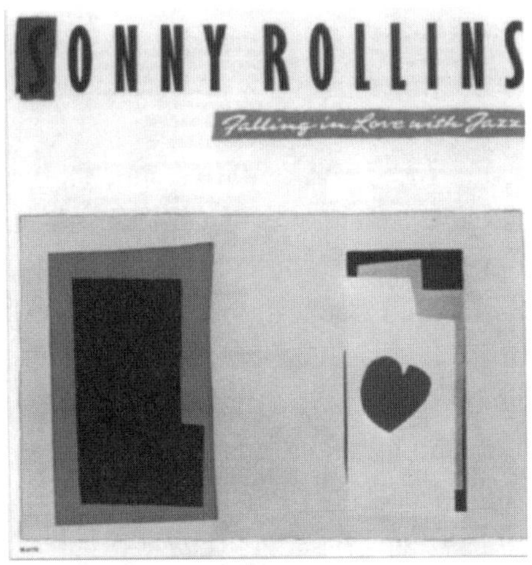

Sonny Rollins (ts) Jerome Harris (g) Mark Soskin (p) Bob Cranshaw (e-b) Jack DeJohnette (dr); New York, 8/5/89:
TENNESSEE WALTZ / LITTLE GIRL BLUE
Same personnel plus Clifton Anderson (tb); New York, 9/9/89:
FALLING IN LOVE WITH LOVE / SISTER AMANDA (only CD)

Parallels with *Sonny Meets Hawk*! are brought to mind. In 1963 Rollins had held a dialogue on the RCA album with his boyhood idol Coleman Hawkins, 26 years his senior. Now an unmistakably Rollins-inspired Branford Marsalis stands in the studio alongside his three-decades-older exemplar. How different, though, is the stylistic division of roles on these records, 26 years apart! Back then Rollins delivered his iconoclastic commentaries on the tenor great's traditional phrases; now it is the newcomer who embodies the past. Rollins introduces the theme of "For All We Know" in the characteristically rough, rasping tone of his current manner–and Marsalis annotates the melody with the Rollins sound–and Rollins phrases!–of the late '50s. In the double solo that follows, the two play a fascinating game of musical catch, drawing nearer and nearer to each other. But then, after Tommy Flanagan's piano solo, their differences emerge again. Marsalis' skillfully constructed chorus practically plagiarizes old Rollins patterns. Rollins, for his part, wants no part of such reverence and nostalgia. In his solo, he dissolves the harmonic and rhythmic contours of the theme into wildly fragmented sound surfaces–as if meaning to show his disciple that being true to oneself does not mean coming to a musical standstill. A fascinating encounter, not only between two generations, but between two interpretations of what tradition means to jazz.

The four (or five, on CD) tracks without Branford Marsalis also feature Rollins at his best: in an acrobatic dismantling of Broadway melodies ("Falling in Love With Love") and tongue-in-cheek approach to most un-jazzlike material ("Tennessee Waltz"). He is supported (another happy circumstance) by first-rate sidemen, particularly Jerome Harris, who had until then excelled as a bass player. Playing creative and unclichéd guitar, Harris follows Rollins into every corner of his stylistic world: from a droll imitation of slide guitar on "Tennessee Waltz," tricky neo-bop lines on "Falling in Love With Love," to the raw sound experiments on the contemporary funk of "Sister." *Falling in Love With Jazz* is a definitive statement on the 40th anniversary of Rollins' recording debut: a declaration of his love for jazz that is respectful of, but not shackled by, tradition.

Sonny Rollins
Here's to the People
Milestone MCD-9194-2
Sonny Rollins (ts) Clifton Anderson (tb) Mark Soskin (p) Jerome Harris (g) Bob Cranshaw (e-b) Steve Jordan (dr); New York, 8/10/91:
HERE'S TO THE PEOPLE / LUCKY DAY
Same personnel, but Jack DeJohnette (dr); New York, 8/17/91:
DOC PHIL
Sonny Rollins (ts) Mark Soskin (p) Jerome Harris (g) Bob Cranshaw (e-b) Steve Jordan (dr); New York, 8/2491:
WHY WAS I BORN? / SOMEONE TO WATCH OVER ME / LONG AGO AND FAR AWAY
Sonny Rollins (ts) Roy Hargrove (tp) Mark Soskin (p) Bob Cranshaw (e-b) Al Foster (dr); New York, 8//91
I WISH I KNEW / YOUNG ROY

"Roy is a guy who has done his homework, he knows his tradition. So I did a concert with him one time and the guys in the band were all about ten years older than Roy. I said 'Let's play this tune,' an old standard called 'I Wish I Knew.' And Roy knew it. The other guys in my band didn't! So I shouldn't say that the young guys don't know these tunes, this tradition, because some of them do. The better young guys know the jazz repertoire." (Nisenson 2000, 207) This anecdote proves that the inclusion of young trumpet lion Roy Hargrove was more than a mere marketing ploy. In the ballad "I Wish I Knew" and the up-tempo number "Young Roy" (a Rollins original like "Doc Phil" and the album's title track), Rollins engages in real dialogue with the trumpeter, an honor

rarely enjoyed by other horn players. Hargrove seems a little timid in "I Wish I Knew"—who wouldn't be intimidated by Rollins' larger-than-life-presence?—but seems more at ease in the exchanges in "Young Roy." But the most stunning title on this spirited album is the Jerome Kern composition "Why Was I Born," a non-stop tenor feature. This is Rollins as he is rarely heard in the studio, inspired and risk-taking from the first second to the last, in a tour de force of melodic invention, harmonic ingenuity, rhythmic energy, and sheer joy—a marvel of the art of improvisation that should convince even the most ardent fan of Rollins' '50s recordings that the gentle giant was still going strong in the '90s.

Sonny Rollins
Old Flames
Milestone MCD-9215-2

Sonny Rollins (ts) Clifton Anderson (tb) Tommy Flanagan (p) Bob Cranshaw (b, e-b) Jack DeJohnette (dr); New York, July/ August 1993:
WHERE OR WHEN / MY OLD FLAME / TIMES SLIMES / I SEE YOUR FACE BEFORE ME / DELIA
Same personnel, plus brass choir (Jon Faddis, Byron Stripling (flh) Alex Brofsky (frh) Bob Stewart (tu); New York, July/August 1993:
DARN THAT DREAM / PRELUDE TO A KISS

A Sonny Rollins ballad album–an overdue idea, one might suppose, and one that could reconcile fans of the "old" Rollins to his more recent work. The execution, however, falls somewhat short of the worthy intentions. Of course, Rollins is a master balladeer, magisterial on classic melodies like Jimmy van Heusen's "Darn That Dream" or Ellington's "Prelude to a Kiss" (the more lively "Times Slimes," the only Rollins original

on this disc, is intended as a musical critique of the *New York Times*, a paper, Rollins feels, marred by journalistic bias). It is hard to sustain an inspired ballad performance for eight or nine minutes, and more often than not, the rhythm section plods. Also, in a transparent musical context like this, the shortcomings of Bob Cranshaw's one-dimensional bass timbre and the difficulties of capturing Rollins' rich saxophone sound with a microphone attached to the tenor's bell become more obvious than usual. Jimmy Heath's "brass choir" arrangements on "Darn That Dream" and "Prelude to a Kiss" make for some timbral variety, but they are not well integrated with the quartet.

Sonny Rollins
Sonny Rollins +3
Milestone MCD 9250-2
Sonny Rollins (ts) Stephen Scott (p) Bob Cranshaw (e-b) Jack

DeJohnette (dr); New York, 8/30/95:
THEEY SAY IT'S WONDERFUL / CABIN IN THE SKY
Sonny Rollins (ts) Tommy Flanagan (p) Bob Cranshaw (e-b) Al Foster (dr); New York, 10/7/95:
WHAT A DIFFERENCE A DAY MADE / BIJI / MONA LISA / H.S. / I'VE NEVER BEEN IN LOVE BEFORE

The album title brings back memories of the '50s, and evokes memories of classic Rollins LPs like *Sonny Rollins + 4*. Save for the Rollins originals "Biji" and "H.S.," the repertoire is retrospective, too, and even the line-up goes back a long way: Flanagan was the pianist on *Saxophone Colossus*, and both Flanagan and Cranshaw participated on the 1965 live date *There Will Never Be Another You*. However, this is also the CD debut of Rollins' collaboration with Steven Scott, his preferred pianist to this day. And if you listen closely to this CD, you will discover not only the similarities of the mid-90s Rollins with 50's Newk, but also the differences. And these differences are by no means negative, as some hard-core nostalgiacs would have it. True, Rollins timbre has changed with the years, and the somewhat gritty sound of recent Rollins may be an acquired taste. True, the not-so-young saxophonist on this recording has trouble controlling his vibrato in the ballad selections, and, on "Cabin In the Sky," there's noticeable difficulty with the instrument's high end. But consider "H.S.," a homage to hard-bop legend Horace Silver (another musician haunted by his glorious past). The theme with its catchy hookline, ending on a descending fifth, is pure hard bop, and in his solo, Rollins plays some of the archetypal percussive phrases that were his hallmark in hard bop's heyday. But then there are also sheets-of-sound departures from the beat, free harmonic investigations, short bursts of pure energy playing that prove that Rollins has drastically expanded his rhythmic and melodic/harmonic vocabulary since the good old days. And listen to how the funk sections of "Biji," one of the more memorable recent Rollins tunes, inspire Tommy Flanagan to some very fresh playing, and how beautifully Jack DeJohnette interacts with the leader on "They Say It's Wonderful." Yes, there are more than enough reasons for the old Rollins fans to like this album. But that doesn't by any means prove that *Sonny Rollins +3* is nostalgic.

Sonny Rollins
Global Warming
Milestone MCD-9280-2
Sonny Rollins (ts) Stephen Scott (p) Bob Cranshaw (e-b) Idris Muhammad (dr); New York, 1/7/98:
ECHO-SIDE BLUE / MOTHER NATURE'S BLUES / CHANGE PARTNERS
Sonny Rollins (ts) Clifton Anderson (tb) Stephen Scott (p) Bob Cranshaw (e-b) Victor See Yuen (perc) Perry Wilson (dr); New York, 2/28/98:
ISLAND LADY / GLOBAL WARMING / CLEAR-CUT BOOGIE

"We got to stop assumin' / We can just go on consumin' / Clean up the air, clean up the food. / Forget that arrogant attitude. / Live light on the planet, sister and brother /'Cause if we kill it, there ain't no other. / Not that much time left neither."

Rollins' poem, printed on the cover of this CD, lays out the ecological message that's been one of his main concerns in recent years. This is the first time since *Freedom Suite* that Rollins has issued an album that invites interpretation as a political statement. The music, however, has little of this somber tone. Quite the contrary, it is light-hearted, sometimes a little lightweight. The joyous, simple theme of "Island Lady" (known from the 1976 LP *The Way I Feel*) is stated a few times too often for its own good, and the thematic content of "Clear-Cut Boogie" (a basic riff tune) and the calypso that gives the CD its name are slight. The extended bass solo in "Island Lady" lacks the momentum of fresh ideas, and in Irving Berlin's "Change Partners" (the only non-Rollins melody on the album) the exchanges between Rollins and drummer Idris Muhammad go on a too long to sustain interest.

But while *Global Warming* may not quite have the musical substance one expects of a meaningful musical-political statement, it does offer its own joys. What a great R&B player Rollins is, as funky as King Curtis, but always escaping from shop-worn phrases into uncharted territory: "Island Lady" offers ample proof. His pitch choices can be unorthodox, almost perversely preferring "wrong" notes but making them sound right by the inner logic of his phrases: the extended "Mother Nature's Blues" is a case in point, and more than compensates for the less interesting cuts on the album. Hardly less memorable: Stephen Scott's inventive blues deconstruction on the same track. The last number, "Clear-Cut Boogie," ends in a long diminuendo, after which Rollins' voice is heard to intone: "...and then there were none." A pessimistic coda to an otherwise rather innocuous album.

Sonny Rollins
This Is What I Do
Milestone MCD-9310-2

Sonny Rollins (ts) Clifton Anderson (tb) Stephen Scott (p) Bob Cranshaw (e-b) Jack DeJohnette (dr); New York, 5/8–9/2000:
SALVADOR / SWEET LEILANI / A NIGHTINGALE SANG IN BERKELEY SQUARE / THE MOON OF MANAKOORA
Same lineup, but Perry Wilson (dr); New York, 7/29/2000:
DID YOU SEE HAROLD VICK? / CHARLES M.

"I've been playing form music. So I want to play logically, according to a form. Because if it's off, then I can't do my thing. Because I'm playing according to time; regardless of what I'm playing, I know where the time is." In the liner notes to the box set *Silver City* (discussed below), Rollins makes a clear distinction between "form music" and "phrase music"—the latter being improvised music not confined by song structures. Rollins certainly experimented with the latter approach in the '60s, but at some point he made his choice: to remain a "form music" improviser, a song player. Yes, Sonny Rollins knows exactly what he's doing, and why he's doing it. And he also knows what this implies in terms of choosing a rhythm section. As he said in the same conversation with liner notes author Chip Stern: "I've always thought that I want to have a steady bass player and a steady rhythm section. Like I did some work in the Sixties with Bob [Cranshaw] and Mickey Roker. When I got those guys to just play steady, then I could sort of play more abstractly. So I've always had this as a modus in a way. Let me get these guys to really know where the beat is and know where the time is, and then I can do the other part." One man's freedom is another man's prison, so to speak: Rollins' flights of imagination work best over the fixed grid of a fairly conventional rhythm section—figure and ground. This is what Sonny Rollins does, and if you don't agree with these aesthetic premises—well, listen to other music and stop pestering Rollins that he should do something different. This may be how to interpret the message inherent in the title *This Is What I Do*. For anyone familiar with Rollins' recordings of the '80s and '90s, the musical menu of this CD will come as no surprise. Catchy Rollins originals like the Caribbean-tinged "Salvador" and the funk-based "Did You See Harold Vick?," a bluesy homage to his old friend Charles Mingus ("Charles M."), a classic ballad ("A Nightingale Sang In Berkeley Square") and one of those unlikely melodies only Sonny Rollins would choose as a vehicle for improvisation ("The Moon of Mankoora"). At 70, Rollins is still in amazing form, physically and mentally. In "Harold Vick," he chooses to solo with bass and drums only—a format he pioneered in the '50s, but which he has avoided for a long time, claiming that it might be too demanding at his age. He need not have worried, that's for sure.

Although both sessions took place in the same studio—Clinton studios in New York, where Rollins has been recording for many years—and although they were engineered by the same person, there is a marked difference in sound. On the May recordings, the tenor sounds warmer and fuller than it has in a long time; on the July takes, it is again the somewhat narrow, mid-rangy sound captured by a microphone attached to the saxophone bell—a sound familiar from many a previous Rollins disc, representing the engineers' attempt to capture the sound of someone who likes to play while moving around.

BOX SETS

Sonny Rollins
The Complete Prestige Recordings
Prestige 7PCD-4407-2

A seven-CD-set containing Rollins' sessions for Bob Weinstock's label in chronological order. No alternate takes, no hitherto unknown titles.

Sonny Rollins
The Freelance Years
The Complete Riverside & Contemporary Recordings
Riverside 5RCD-4427-2

The end of 1956 also saw the end of Rollins' exclusive contract with Prestige. In the three years up to his first sabbatical, he would record prolifically for various labels. This 5-CD set collects his work for Riverside and Contemporary as a leader and sideman, plus a lesser known 1957 quintet date

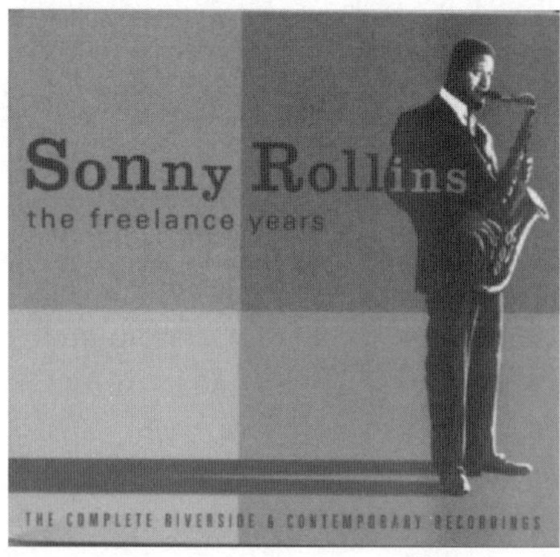

for the short-lived Period label (*Sonny Rollins Plays*). Since this material–apart from the latter session–is readily available on CD, and since this box set, lacking essential Blue Note, Atlantic and Verve recordings of the saxophonist, cannot really provide a representative overview of this most fertile period in Rollins' career, one might question the need for this release. But six hours of prime Rollins, nicely packaged, competently annotated by Zan Stewart with a number of rarely seen photographs, do make a strong collective case in favor of the collection.

Sonny Rollins
The Complete RCA Victor Recordings
RCA Victor 09026-68675-2

This 6-CD set contains the music of the RCA albums *The Bridge, What's New, Our Man In Jazz, Sonny Meets Hawk, Now's the Time* and *The Standard Sonny Rollins,* plus the three quartet tracks (with Don Cherry) originally issued on *3 in Jazz,* and the 1964 titles issued–without Rollins' consent–by the French RCA on the double LP *The Alternative Rollins.* There are no further alternate takes, no previously unknown material. The box includes a lengthy essay by Loren Schoenberg.

Sonny Rollins
Silver City
A Celebration of 25 Years on Milestone
Milestone 2 MCD-2501-2

It was Gary Giddins' plea in a 1995 issue of the *Village Voice* for a reappraisal of Rollins' often-maligned Milestone recordings, and his suggestion that Milestone should compile a best-of sampler from these discs, that gave rise to this collection. The 19 tracks assembled on two CDs do indeed prove two things: that there are many gems on these 20 albums in 25 years; and that the majority of these jewels are to be found in the '80s and '90s releases–for only five tracks of this selection supervised by Sonny and Lucille Rollins come from the '70s albums, while the fourteen remaining were recorded between 1982 and 1995. It is hardly surprising that LPs such as *Horn Culture* and *Nucleus* are passed over, while the more recent (and successful) *Sunny Days, Starry Nights, Dancing In The Dark, Here's to the People,* and *Sonny Rollins + 3* are represented with two tracks each. This is indeed a splendid overview of the period from 1972 to 1995 and highly recommended as an introduction to Rollins' later work. A further bonus: an extended essay by Chip Stern, in which Sonny Rollins sets out his aesthetic credo more explicitly and persuasively than he's ever done before.

abbreviations

arr arranger
as alto saxophone
b bass
bcl bass clarinet
cga conga
cl clarinet
cond conductor
cor cornet
dr drums
e-b electric bass
e-g electric guitar
e-org electric organ
e-perc electric percussion
fl flute
fr-h French horn
g guitar
g-synth guitar synthesizer
key keyboards
ob oboe
org organ
p piano
perc percussion
sax saxophone
ss soprano saxophone
synth synthesizer
tb tuba
ts tenor saxophone
tp trumpet
v violin
va viola
vc cello
vib vibraphone
voc vocal
xyl xylophone

bibliography

Books, book chapters, and encyclopedia articles

Blancq, Charles: *Sonny Rollins: The Journey of a Jazzman* (Boston 1983).

Cole, Bill: *John Coltrane* (New York 1976).

Collier, James Lincoln: *The Making of Jazz. A Comprehensive History* (London, Toronto, Sydney, etc. 1978).

Davis, Francis: "An Improviser Prepares (Sonny Rollins)." In: *In the Moment. Jazz In The 1980s* (New York/Oxford 1986), 117–132.

Davis, Miles and Troupe, Quincy: *The Autobiography* (New York 1989).

Giddins, Gary: *Rhythm-A-Ning. Jazz Tradition And Innovation in The 80's* (New York/Oxford 1985).

Idem, "There's No One Like Sonny Rollins." In: *Riding on a Blue Note. Jazz and American Pop* (New York/Oxford 1981), 120–130.

Goldberg, Joe: "Sonny Rollins." In: *Jazz Masters Of The Fifties* (New York 1965), 87–112 (= Goldberg 1965a).

Jost, Ekkehard: *Free Jazz. Stilkritische Untersuchungen zum Jazz der 60er Jahre* (Mainz 1975).

Kernfeld, Barry (ed.): *The New Grove Dictionary of Jazz* (London 1988).

Kunzler, Martin: *Jazz-Lexikon* (Reinbek 1988).

Litweiler, John: *The Freedom Principle. Jazz After 1958* (New York 1984).

Lyons, Len: *The Great Jazz Pianists. Speaking Of Their Lives And Music* (New York 1983).

Nisenson, Eric: *Open Sky. Sonny Rollins and His World of Improvisation* (New York 2000).

Polillo, Arrigo: "Sonny Rollins." In: *Jazz. Geschichte und Persönlichkeiten* (München/Mainz 1981), 554–566.

Postif, François: "Sonny Rollins" [interview]. In: *Les grandes interviews de Jazz Hot* (Paris 1989), 75–86.

Priestley, Brian: *Mingus. A Critical Biography* (London 1982).

Schuller, Gunther: "Sonny Rollins and the Challenge of Thematic Improvisation." In: *Musings. The Musical Worlds of Gunther Schuller* (New York/Oxford 1986), 86–97 (reprinted from *Jazz Review,* Nov. 1958).

Taylor, Arthur: "Sonny Rollins" [interview]. In: *Notes And Tones. Musician-to-Musician Interviews* (London 1983), 166–174.

Williams, Martin: "Sonny Rollins. Spontaneous Orchestration." In: *The Jazz Tradition.* New And Revised Edition (Oxford/New York 1983), 183–193.

Periodical literature

Belden, Bob: "The Man. Jazz Artist of the Year: Sonny Rollins." *Down Beat,* August 1997, 18–25.

Berg, Chuck: "Sonny Rollins. The Way Newk Feels." *Down Beat*, 4/7/77, 13–14 and 38–41.

Blumenthal, Bob: "The Bridge. Sonny Rollins is a tenor for all times." *Rolling Stone*, 7/12/79, 56f.

Idem: "Sonny Rollins Interview." *Down Beat*, May 1982, 15–18.

Cerulli, Dom: "Theodore Walter Rollins. Sonny Believes He Can Accomplish Much More Than He Has To Date." *Down Beat*, 7/10/58, 16–17.

Childs, Charles: "Sonny Rollins: 'I Welcome Change.' " *Jazz Forum*, January 1980, 29–32.

Cioe, Crispin: "Sonny Rollins: 'I'm Still Reaching'...and still surprising his audiences." *High Fidelity*, May 1983, 76–78, 90.

Cook, Richard: "Sonny Rollins: Return Of The Colossus." *Wire*, August 1985, 28–31.

Cooke, Jack: "Sonny Rollins: Renewing The Spark." *Wire*, November 1986, 18–19, 64.

Coss, Bill: "The Return Of Sonny Rollins." *Down Beat*, 1/4/62, 13f.

Delmas, Jean: "Traditions & Contradictions de Theodore Walter 'Sonny' Rollins." *Jazz Hot*, July–August 1974, 14–17.

Endress, Gudrun: "Kampf ums künstlerische Überleben: Sonny Rollins." *Jazz Podium*, July 1977, 6–9.

Fiofori, Tam: "Re-Entry: The New Orbit Of Sonny Rollins." *Down Beat*, 10/14/71, 14–15, 39.

Giddins, Gary: "Rollins Record Date Spots Soprano Sax." *Down Beat*, 10/12/72, 10.

Gitler, Ira: "Sonny Rollins: Music Is An Open Sky." *Down Beat*, May 1969, 18-19.

Idem: "Caught In The Act." *Down Beat*, 10/3/68, 31.

Goldberg, Joe: "The Further Adventures Of Sonny Rollins." *Down Beat*, 8/26/65, 19–21 (= Goldberg 1965b).

Hadlock, Dick: "Caught In The Act." *Down Beat*, 5/24/62, 41.

Idem: "Heard In Person." *Down Beat*, 12/11/58, 49.

Hultin, Randi: "Caught In The Act." *Down Beat*, 9/16/71, 37–38.

Jarrett, Michael: "Sonny Rollins Interview." *Cadence*, July 1990, 5–8, 28.

Kalbacher, Gene: "Sonny Rollins Interview." *Down Beat*, July 1988, 16–19.

Kirchner, Bill: "Sonny Rollins." *Down Beat*, 6/2/77, 37.

Kopulos, Gordon: "Needed Now: Sonny Rollins." *Down Beat*, 6/24/71, 12–13, 30.

McDonough, John: "Sonny's Side of the Street." *Down Beat*, December 1992, 22–25.

Morgenstern, Dan: "Jazz Goes To Washington." *Musical America*, July 1962, 18–19.

Nicholson, Stuart: "Great Recordings. Sonny Rollins: Saxophone Colossus." *The Wire*, August 1985, 33–35.

Panken, Ted: "Sonny Rollins: Approaching Enlightenment," *Down Beat* 68.2 (February 2001), 22–27.

Porter, Bob: "This Man Called…Sonny." *Down Beat*, 2/14/74, 14–15.

Priestley, Brian: "Sonny Rollins: Dancing In The Lights." *Wire*, June 1988, 32–35.

Russell, ? : "Sabbatical." *The New Yorker*, 11/18/61, 41–42.

West, Hollie I.: "Rollins: Return of a Recluse." *Jazz Forum*, May 1974, 21–24.

Whitehead, Kevin: "When Sonny Gets Mad." *Down Beat*,

January 1995, 16–21.

Williams, Martin: "The Novelist And The Hornman." *Down Beat*, 9/5/68, 14.

Idem: "Composers' Showcase." *Down Beat*, 5/1/69, 37–38.

Discographies

Bruyninckx, W.: *Modern Discography* (Mechelen n.d., 6 vols.).

Sjøgren, Thørbjørn: *The Sonny Rollins Discography* (Copenhagen 1983).

Swing Journal [Japan], April 1990, 220–225.

See also the appendix to Blancq 1983.

Transcriptions

Baker, David N.: *The Jazz Style of Sonny Rollins. A Musical and Historical Perspective* (Hialeah, Fla. 1980) (includes transcriptions of nine solos from between 1951 and 1972 with analytic commentary).

Gerard, Charley: *Jazz Masters: Sonny Rollins* (New York 1987) (contains transcriptions of nine solos from between 1956 and 1972 and a brief "Analysis of Sonny Rollins' Style").

Additional transcriptions in Blancq 1983.

index of albums